ECK Masters and You

An Illustrated Guide

ECK Masters and You

An Illustrated Guide

HAROLD KLEMP

ECKANKAR
Minneapolis
www.Eckankar.org

ECK Masters and You: An Illustrated Guide

Printed in USA

Compiled by Joan Klemp and Sharmaine Wittsack from Harold Klemp's writings and the real-life stories by students of Eckankar published in *The Eckankar Journal*.

Cover art by Don McFadden

Edited by Patrick Carroll and Anthony Moore

Second printing—2006

Library of Congress Cataloging-in-Publication Data

Klemp, Harold.
    ECK masters and you : an illustrated guide / Harold Klemp.
        p. cm.
    ISBN 1-57043-228-7 (pbk : alk. paper)
       1. Eck masters. 2. Spiritual life--Eckankar (Organization) I. Title.
    BP605.E3K5537 2006
    299'.93--dc22
                                         2005032070

♾ This paper meets the requirements of ANSI/NISO Z39.48-1992 (Permanence of Paper).

Contents

Who Are
the ECK Masters?

Who Are the ECK Masters?

Don McFadden

The ECK Masters are spiritual guides people have looked to since the beginning of time for guidance, protection, and divine love. By the way, "ECK" means the Holy Spirit.

The ECK Masters walk among you now, today, ready to encourage Soul on Its journey home to God.

You are Soul. It is the real you.

You are a timeless, deathless spark of God—in love, strength, and beauty—upheld by the always present Light and Sound, the Holy Spirit.

Every person has a chance to find spiritual freedom. The ECK Masters light up an event, a dream, or an unusual encounter to clear the way.

They often come in people's dreams, while at other times they offer aid in our daily lives.

There are lots of stories about the many occasions one of the ECK Masters or the Mahanta, the Inner Master, has helped an individual with healing, protection, or an outpouring of divine love.

The ECK Masters help all who really want to find the true love and wisdom that is their divine heritage.

This book offers a brief introduction to the ECK Masters and how these Co-workers with God can help you.

Rebazar Tarzs

Tibetan Adept and Torchbearer of Eckankar

Rebazar Tarzs

Rebazar Tarzs *(REE-bah-zahr TAHRZ)* is the Torchbearer of Eckankar in the lower worlds. He was the spiritual teacher of many ECK Masters. Said to be over five hundred years old, Rebazar Tarzs lives in a hut in the Hindu Kush Mountains and appears to many as he helps the current Living ECK Master in the works of Eckankar.

Betsy White

The Travelers of ECK

The first ECK Master I met on the inner planes was Paul Twitchell, whose spiritual name is Peddar Zaskq. The next most important ECK Traveler I met was the beloved Rebazar Tarzs. Rebazar is a Tibetan who served as the leader of the ECK community many years ago, when Tibet was the spiritual center of the world and the teachings were taught in secret.

Rebazar is almost six feet in height. His beard is as thick as black wool and neatly trimmed. His hands are big and square, testimony to the rugged outdoor life he enjoys. Someone who meets him during Soul Travel sees a strong, deeply tanned traveler who is master of every possible situation.

Ann Hubert

His knowledge of the Far Country is extraordinary, and he has given his whole life to helping others find the perfection of God.

Another feature of Rebazar worth noting is his eyes. Like two dark pools in a bottomless sea, they seem to see all, know all. They are eyes of compassion and mercy, all-seeing eyes that serve both as a mirror of Soul and a microscope to the universe. To look into them is to become lost in the Sound and Light of God, the ECK. The liquid of God pours from them like a sweet nectar to fill the emptiness of the heart, and I drank deeply when we met in the spiritual worlds.

This is a fair description of Rebazar Tarzs. He and all the other ECK Masters are Co-workers with the Living ECK Master, who during my term as an ECK novice was Paul Twitchell.

The ECK Travelers are coaches, not mediators; does anyone dare come between God and man? They advise people of the best way to God. A football coach gives his players the advantage of his own years of experience as a player, in addition to all he has learned since then, but the players take the bruises on the field. After all, it's their game. A good coach will see to it that they reach the goal line as quickly and easily as possible.

It is hard to talk about the Far Country because of the limits of human expression. The experiences that take place there have their own language. Yet perhaps the meetings described in the pages that follow will show how the ECK Travelers help people with the burdens of their heart.

Rebazar Shares a Divine Secret

They saw the maroon-robed figure of the Traveler standing among the trees. He came forward and spoke, "Ah, I must speak with thee, my friends. This is the night to tell thee of the loving heart.

"Ye know that the greatest of God's qualities is love. For love is the greatest and most sublime force of the universe. Through love the divine qualities of God will shine like the radiant light of the morning sun.

"I will whisper to thee, dear ones, this divine secret. Let thine ears become filled with wisdom and thy hearts with understanding. Now it is this: All things will gravitate to thee if ye will let love enter thine own hearts, without compromise."

— ECK Master Rebazar Tarzs speaking to the seeker and his beloved, as recorded in *Stranger by the River* by Paul Twitchell

Signy Cohen

A Seeker Is Born

A young man in Africa was twenty-two, and he had all kinds of financial problems. He also had a serious health problem: his eyesight was failing.

He said, "God, please take me from this vale of tears. I have had as much as I can take of this physical world." He prayed that every night.

One night he was taken out of the body, perhaps in a way similar to Paul, the apostle, who said he was caught up even unto the third heaven. The young man fell asleep on his bed, and the next thing he knew, he was in another world. It was a very beautiful place. The temperature was just right, and there was an enormous amount of light. Everything had a clarity and a refreshing goodness about it that was filled with love and compassion. "I like this place," he said. "I would like to stay here."

There was a hut nearby, and two men stepped out of it. One of the men had a thick, black beard. Much later, after this experience, the young man would recognize this person as the ECK Master Rebazar Tarzs. But at the time he had no idea who this man was or where he was.

The man with the black beard said to him, "Why are you here?"

The young African said, "I'm here because I'm sick of Earth and this is a nice place. I think I'd like to stay here with you." He explained his prayer to God. He said, "I've been praying to God to get me away from Earth, and it looks as if it's worked. I think I'd like to stay."

As he looked around at the clear blue sky, he happened to notice a light coming from the little hut. It was a blue light, but it didn't seem to be coming from a single source. It seemed to be emanating from everywhere at once. He didn't know this was the Light of God, often known as the Blue Light of the Mahanta.

The man with the black beard said to him, "You can't stay. You have to go back."

The young man said, "No, I won't go back. I shall stay." He went through all his reasons again of why he wanted to stay in this place of love and beauty.

The ECK Master told him, "It's impossible because you haven't finished your mission on Earth."

The young man said, "That may be, but I'm not going back."

The ECK Master came over to him very kindly and took hold of his hand, and the next thing the young man knew, he was back in his room waking up. He sat up in his bed, and he said, "What was that?"

He had become the seeker.

This young African went to his priest and began asking questions. He wanted to know what this experience meant. Where was this place of love and beauty? While he was there in this other world, Rebazar Tarzs had asked him, "Do you know where you are?"

The young man did not have a clue. He simply said, "I don't care. It's a good place. I think I'll stay."

The priest had no answer as to where this place was or what it meant. But the experience

Signy Cohen

gave the young man hope. He no longer prayed to God to remove him from this physical world because of all his hardships. He didn't know what his mission was yet, but he did know that he hadn't completed it. So he began a search, and in time he came across some ECK books and began reading them.

In one of the ECK books he found a picture of the ECK Master Rebazar Tarzs. The young seeker recognized him immediately as the man who had met him outside the little hut in the other worlds.

The Fire of God's Love

April Munson

After an ECK initiate had the experience in his spiritual exercise of hearing crickets and the sound of rockets, he realized he had to give more time to the Spiritual Exercises of ECK. He had to take them one step further.

When the next experience began, he found himself out of the physical body and in the Soul consciousness. He was very aware; he knew that he could be anywhere in the universes just by wanting to be. You become the wish fulfilled. And the way you become the wish fulfilled is you think of something or someone that you very much want to see.

This ECKist wanted to see the ECK Master Rebazar Tarzs.

Rebazar Tarzs lives up in the Hindu Kush Mountains, but most of his service is among people in the cities and in the crowds. He meets you where you need to meet him, when the time is right. And so this individual awoke on the other planes in full consciousness, in the Soul consciousness, out in the Soul body, and he found himself on the side of a steep mountain. First he saw the snow on distant mountaintops. And then he saw the nearby mountains.

He was standing on a ridge. He looked around, wondering, *Where is Rebazar?* And then he filled his heart with love, because he knew he had to give love if he wanted to take this experience a step further. So he just felt a strong, strong love for this ancient ECK Master.

There was the sound of footsteps off to the side, and coming along the ridge trail was Rebazar Tarzs.

"I'm happy to see you," Rebazar said. "Let's build a fire." It was cold. The ECKist looked around and found a few twigs from nearby bushes. He and Rebazar gathered a small pile alongside the ridge on this mountain. And Rebazar reached into his robe and pulled out a little bottle of paraffin. He poured this over the twigs and put a light to it. Immediately there was a bright flame.

If you ignite paraffin, it makes a brief, hot flame. But just as quickly as it starts, the fire dies out. After the flames died, only a few embers were left of the fire on the ridge trail.

As the ECK initiate watched, Rebazar Tarzs bent over this little fire and very carefully blew on the embers. Then he fed twigs into the fire, and very slowly they ignited. Soon there was a real fire going.

Rebazar Tarzs told him, "Often, when a person first comes into ECK, he has this strong hot flame of experiences. He will have many psychic experiences, and he will feel this is the real thing. But as they pass, as the mind forgets, the doubts return. And then the ECKist wonders, *Were those experiences real? Did these things really happen to me?*

"But the Master keeps blowing on these embers and uses the base of these experiences to build on. In time the ECKist, the God seeker, finds within him this slow burning, long-lasting love for God."

A seeker's own personal experiences in the Light and Sound of God prove the validity of the ECK teachings. In the following two accounts of meeting the ECK Master Rebazar Tarzs, students of Eckankar tell their experience in their own words.

A Visit from an ECK Master

A Special Spiritual Message
Saved This Ecuadoran Woman's Life

MONICA RIVERA

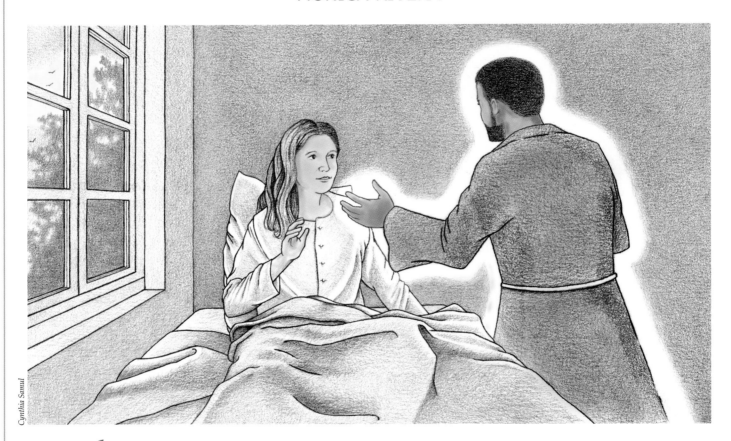

Cynthia Samul

*I*f you want to survive," boomed the deep voice of my visitor, "you must follow my instructions. As soon as the sun rises, you must go to the bus stop."

A heart attack had forced me to quit my job, and after fifteen days in bed, I was as weak as a kitten, unable to do anything for myself. I stared in disbelief at the bearded stranger by my bedside. Who was he? Where had he come from?

Strangely I felt no fear. The beautiful energy that radiated from him was familiar. I had felt that comforting presence at my side day and night since I had fallen ill.

"The bus stop is seven blocks away," I protested. "How will I ever get there?"

"If you want to survive, you must go now," came his reply. "Walk slowly. Catch the bus to Santo Domingo Plaza."

Again I asked, "How can I walk seven blocks in this condition?"

Brushing my protest

Mar Amongo

aside, he repeated his command, "You must go now!" Then he was gone.

I dragged myself out of bed and struggled into my clothes. All the way to the bus stop I fought to stay on my feet, shaking and sweating profusely. But every time I faltered, I heard my benefactor's voice: "Keep going, keep going." Finally I reached the bus stop.

When the bus to Santo Domingo Plaza arrived, I felt a steadying arm help me aboard. There was no one in sight.

At my destination, I exited the bus and began to walk slowly across the plaza as I had been instructed. My inner guide spoke again. "Sit and rest on that bench for a few minutes. Then resume walking up the hill. Be alert. There is a man on his way down who has what you need."

After resting a bit, I continued on. I was ready to collapse, when I saw a small

Indian man, about fifty years old, clad in a red poncho, a round white hat, and short white pants. He was carrying a small basket. He had a beautiful face.

Heading down the hill straight toward me, the vendor cried, "Herbs for your heart! Herbs for your heart!" I tried to hurry toward him, but the pain in my chest made it impossible to go any further. I waited anxiously for him to reach me.

"Grandpa, how much for all your herbs and the basket to carry it in?" I asked.

"One centavo," he replied sweetly. I could scarcely believe my ears. I wanted to hug him, but I knew it would be unseemly. Instead I placed my arm on his shoulder and thanked him profusely. I was so grateful. But my effort had weakened me even further, so I sat down on the curb, hugging my lifesaving basket. I turned to wave one more thank-you, but the little man had disappeared.

After a long and difficult journey home, I prepared the herbs and began to take them. In eight days, my heart was completely healed. I began to exercise to regain my strength and was back at work twenty days later.

All this happened many, many years ago. Years later, after I joined Eckankar, I discovered the identity of my black-bearded, maroon-robed savior—the ECK Master Rebazar Tarzs! He had sat invisibly by my bed throughout my illness and directed me to the mysterious vendor whose herbs saved my life.

Encounter with an ECK Master

MI JA COYLE

Many years ago, my husband and I traveled to a large city to meet with a long-time member of Eckankar. We had become very interested in Eckankar after my husband had found an ECK book in our local library. Now we wanted to talk to someone who had experience with it.

When we arrived, we were met with much love and warmth. We were shown to the ECKist's living room. On the wall was a large painting of a man with black hair and short beard wearing a maroon robe. He was standing with one foot in a small boat and the other foot on the rocky shore. His

Mar Amongo

hand reached out, as welcoming as his wonderful smile.

I recognized him at once. I had known him during my childhood and searched for him ever since. Now, twenty-five years later, here was a painting of him.

Old memories I had long forgotten started coming back. My heart was pounding with excitement.

As soon as we were back in the car, I asked my husband who the dark-haired man in the painting was.

"He's Rebazar Tarzs, one of the ECK Masters. Why?"

"That man saved my family's lives during the Korean War," I replied, as the memories came flooding back. It was so exciting, as if it had happened only a few days ago.

The war had been going on for months. We were trying to get away from the North Korean soldiers and stay away from the combat zones. My brothers and sisters and I were constantly hungry, sometimes walking for many days without food, hoping to find a safe place to rest.

At last we made our way into the south, away from the fighting. There were so many people and no food or water. My parents soon found their money was worthless. Those who had extra food wanted clothes or blankets in exchange.

During the bombing of our home, we had had only enough time to dress and take our soon-to-be-useless money with us. A blanket or coat would have been worth much more.

Bo Coyle

He took off his jacket and handed it to me. "Trade this for the food you need," he said.

We were all alive and together, but slowly starving and unbelievably tired. All the rules of our society had changed, and we just didn't know how to survive in this new arena of war. Our hunger forced my parents to go out on longer and longer searches for food and water or things that could be traded for food. One day I felt I needed to go with my mother on her daily search. She told me to hold on to her skirt and not let go, no matter what happened.

Everywhere we went, there were people and children crying. I grew tired, but my mother told me that if I fell the people would take me away. I don't know how far we walked,

but that fear kept me going.

By the end of the day, I was so weary I stumbled and almost fell. When I looked up, I saw two big boots in front of me. Then I gazed into the eyes of a big dark man in a strange uniform.

For a moment fear clutched me. But the love from his eyes was so beautiful and peaceful.

A smile spread across his broad face. My weakness disappeared. As we stood there in war-torn Korea, he said in a strange language, "You will be all right." Yet I understood each word. Who was this man? My mother, unmoving and silent, stared in awe. The man took off his jacket and handed it to me. "Trade this for the food you need," he said. I nodded my understanding, took my mother's hand, and headed back to our family.

As we walked away I turned to look once more at his love-filled eyes. But he was gone! He was too tall to disappear so quickly among the people around us. Yet he was nowhere to be seen. I remember having such a deep sense of loss—for someone I didn't even know.

Since my childhood, I had often wondered about that wonderful man. Now, after finding Eckankar, I can visit with him again from time to time.

I know that Divine Spirit and the ECK Masters have been protecting and guiding me for a long time. They have been there for me not only in times of suffering but also in times of joy.

Spiritual Exercise
Beach Walk with Rebazar

If you would like to try a Soul Travel exercise, here is an easy one that should let you meet the ECK Master Rebazar Tarzs or enjoy a short journey into the heavens of God.

Picture yourself on a beach, walking in the sand at the edge of the water. The warm waves wash about your feet, and a light spray from the ocean leaves a refreshing mist on your face. Overhead, white gulls sail silently on the wind.

Now breathe in as the incoming waves wash toward you on the beach. Then, on the outgoing breath, sing *Rebazar* (REE-bah-zahr) softly in rhythm with the waves returning to the sea. Do this exercise for twenty to thirty minutes every day. After you are skilled at this exercise, Rebazar will come and give you the wisdom of God.

If you live near the seashore, walk along the beach to get a feeling of the sounds of the ocean. Or imagine the feeling of sand under your feet, the ocean spray, and the many blue-green waters that reach the horizon. Use your impressions from the seashore in your daily Soul Travel exercise.

At first, you may feel that you have only met Rebazar in your imagination, but in time and with practice, you will find that he is every bit a flesh-and-blood individual, even as you are.

You may not see Rebazar or another ECK Master on your short Soul Travel journey, but someone is always near to lend a hand, should you need it.

Merrill Peterson

Yaubl Sacabi

Guardian of the Shariyat-Ki-Sugmad
at the Spiritual City of Agam Des

Yaubl Sacabi

Yaubl Sacabi (*YEEOW-buhl sah-KAH-bee*) was the ECK Master among the Mycenaeans (invaders of Greece between 2000–1700 BC). He was the leading figure among the Greek mystery cults and is now the guardian of the Shariyat-Ki-Sugmad, the sacred book of ECK, in the spiritual city of Agam Des, home of the Eshwar-Khanewale, the God-eaters.

Ann Hubert

The Useless Son

A seven-year-old girl felt useless, unloved, and unwanted. Her family life was not very happy, but the bigger problem was how she felt about herself.

That summer she began meeting in her dreams with an ECK Master who identified himself as Yaubl Sacabi.

One time they met in the desert near a small encampment. A desert storm began to blow up, and people ran for shelter. Nearby she saw a little man trying to get some camels to move, but they wouldn't budge.

The man began to curse the camels, and he

Dick Graham

began to curse his son. "Where is that useless son, Yaubl?" he said. "I had hoped he'd take over the family business and make something of himself. But he's always off with his head in the clouds."

The girl stood by Yaubl Sacabi watching his father in the distance trying to get the camels into shelter from the dust storm. His father was calling him useless, even as the little girl felt useless and unwanted.

And as Yaubl stood there he explained to her, "Everything I have I will always give to anyone else who needs it." It wasn't until years later that she read similar words in *The Shariyat-Ki-Sugmad* and understood what Yaubl Sacabi was saying.

Yaubl spoke to her in her dreams many times as a child. He always had to speak above the angry scolding of his father. Yaubl explained the spiritual wisdom of ECK to this little girl who also felt useless and unwanted. Many years later, as an adult, she found the ECK teachings.

On the inner planes, the ECK Masters, these great spiritual beings, come to help each person as that individual needs it at that very moment, regardless of age.

They will help all who want the gift of spiritual understanding.

Dick Graham

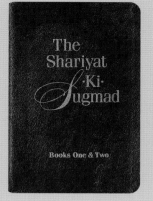

Book Two of *The Shariyat-Ki-Sugmad* was dictated by Yaubl Sacabi, the great ECK Master who serves at the Gare-Hira Temple of Golden Wisdom at Agam Des in the Hindu Kush Mountains.

Spiritual City of Agam Des

Guardian and Teacher

In the remote, hidden spiritual city of Agam Des, Yaubl Sacabi is guardian of the portion of the Shariyat-Ki-Sugmad found there. The city is also home to the Eshwar-Khanewale, a mysterious brotherhood known as the God-eaters, because they consume cosmic energy instead of material food. It is the reason they live to ages well beyond the average span of life.

Entrance to the city is by invitation alone, and then only in the Soul body.

You will recognize Yaubl at first sight, for his bald head looks a bit like a brass dome. A strong nose, thick neck, and well-developed muscles in arms and chest outline a capable, rugged appearance. And you soon find that he takes great pleasure in teaching you and others the secret laws of life, which give new meaning to our existence here.

Gare-Hira is the fourth major Temple of Golden Wisdom on the physical plane. It lies secluded in the remote Hindu Kush, in the spiritual city of Agam Des, and this is where Yaubl Sacabi is guardian and teacher.

The Temple of Gare-Hira is a white structure somewhat like an Islamic mosque, a sturdy building with a white dome topped by a cupola. Classrooms ring the main sanctuary. And lodged in this temple is the second section of the Shariyat-Ki-Sugmad, displayed upon the altar of the inner sanctum. The title of this section is "The Records of the Kros." As already stated, the ECK Master Yaubl Sacabi is the head teacher here, and students come nightly, by invitation, in their Soul forms, to study the ancient wisdom of God.

And what is the essence of Yaubl Sacabi's teaching? It is that the lot of each individual is to become a Co-worker with God, which brings to him the joys of wisdom, charity, and spiritual freedom.

Dick Graham

A Visit to Agam Des

Sara loved to read about people's experiences with Soul Travel. It was fascinating how the ECK Masters would meet neophyte travelers in their dreams and take them to a Temple of Golden Wisdom. She'd read many such stories in the ECK books and publications.

Sara practiced the Spiritual Exercises of ECK every day. She eagerly looked forward to having her own experiences within the grand universes of creation.

One day in contemplation, she arrived at a room that looked a bit like an ancient chapel. Three long, low steps at the front of the room led up to an alcove underneath a large marble arch, beyond

Yaubl Sacabi

Betsy White

ECK Masters and You

embrace. She desperately wanted to approach the lectern.

Disappointment welled up within her. Yet she realized it would do well to obey the precept. At the same time, however, she felt a warm and loving grace lull her troubled mind.

Then a thought flashed in her mind: God had spoken to her! And even better, she'd heard and understood. It had whispered through the knowing voice in her heart. Without the least hesitation, she'd actually grasped the meaning of the strange script. She'd instinctively known what it said.

While she stood pondering the divine benevolence, a bald man in a short white robe appeared off to one side of the alcove, beneath the arch. Sara recognized him. It was the ECK Master Yaubl Sacabi. A most beautiful, mellow golden countenance and extraordinary brown eyes smiled in greeting. His eyes were warm and electric. He motioned her to mount the steps and enter the alcove. There, Yaubl Sacabi began to teach her the secrets of how to commune with the sacred scriptures.

which stood a lectern, with an open book upon it.

Sara's eyes grew large. There was a strong possibility that this place might be a Temple of Golden Wisdom, and that the open book upon the lectern was the famed Shariyat-Ki-Sugmad. What an amazing find!

But something caught her eye.

High above the steps, on the marble archway, there was strange writing. It was in the script of a language she'd never heard or seen, featuring unusual marks like those of some ancient hieroglyphics. Sara had a haunting feeling that she instinctively understood its meaning.

A weight of unhappiness dropped upon her, because the message said, "Please do not come up here unless you have been invited."

Sara knew that the precious books of the Shariyat-Ki-Sugmad contain the wisdom of the ages—the secrets of ECK that she so longed to

Miracle Healing at Five

Hit-and-Run Brings an ECK Master into My Life

JOHN TAY

Suddenly a soft, beautiful blue light enveloped my foot.

When I was five, I loved playing football. One day after a game, as I ran across the road on my way home, a car ran over my left foot. I looked in horror at my foot. No one heard my screams; the driver of the car had driven off, oblivious to the accident.

I sat alone, alongside the road next to the gutter, moaning in pain. How was I ever going to get home?

Suddenly a soft, beautiful blue light enveloped my foot. At the same time, I heard a comforting voice: "Don't worry, the pain will go away."

At the tender age of five, I accepted this assurance with joy and innocence. I got up and walked home.

When I got home and my old uncle saw the torn flesh on my foot, he shouted in alarm. Quick as lightning, he poured half a bottle of iodine on the wound. The pain was so intense that I fainted.

While unconscious, I saw a bald man dressed in a maroon robe standing beside me, peering at my injured foot. In the same voice that I had heard by the roadside, he advised me to wash my foot with clean water. "You will be all right," he said gently.

When I opened my eyes, I was sure I must have been dreaming. There was no one in the room with me. I crept into the bathroom and gently cleaned the wound with cold water from the tap as I had been instructed. All the while, I could feel some unseen force guiding my hand. The soft blue light once again whirled around my poor foot. I felt loved and lighthearted.

Before long, the foot had healed and the skin was back to normal. It was only many years later that I learned the bald man who had healed my foot was the ECK Master Yaubl Sacabi. He had protected me for many years before I found Eckankar!

My Adventure into Life
Patience and Persistence Leads to Soul Travel Success

BIODUN AKINTOLA

Soul Travel was one of the high points that attracted me to the teachings of Eckankar. I had always known it was possible to be out of my body. But how? I didn't know until I came across Eckankar late in 1984 and started attending an ECK book discussion class.

I had a strong desire to travel in the Soul body, but the harder I tried, the more frustrated I became. Nothing seemed to be happening. Yet I persisted.

One Saturday afternoon in January 1985, while alone in my bedroom, I decided to give Soul Travel another try. I lay on my back in bed, closed my eyes, and began to sing HU, an ancient love song to God.

After a while, I felt my heart opening. Then a rushing wind. My physical body seemed to dissolve as I was lifted out of it. I became aware that I was flying high in the sky, feeling the presence of the Inner Master riding on the wind with me.

Suddenly I was afraid. I stopped singing HU. Inwardly, I shouted to the Inner Master, "Mahanta, Mahanta, bring me down." But he encouraged me to keep going until we came to a brilliant white city and entered a domed, glowing-white building. Inside, a bald, rugged-looking man welcomed me, encouraging me to feel free to return anytime.

At once, I was back in my physical body. Later in my ECK studies I recognized this being as Yaubl Sacabi, head of the spiritual city of Agam Des. I had traveled to Agam Des without even knowing of its existence!

This first experience in Soul Travel taught me to keep my fear in check. Fear had robbed me of the full conscious enjoyment of this experience. Fifteen years later, I am more comfortable with Soul Travel. I no longer resist when this phenomenon is at the rim of my consciousness. I just flow along with one of the ECK Masters who has come to take me on a spiritual journey.

Dick Graham

We came to a brilliant white city and entered a domed, glowing-white building.

Valerie Taglieri

Messenger for God

Singing HU Brings an Unexpected Meeting with an ECK Master

WINNIE MAA

I often travel because of my job, staying in a different hotel almost every night. I always carry pictures of ECK Masters and ECK books for reading and sharing with others. And wherever I travel, I tell people about singing HU.

Late one night I was packing for a seventeen-hour flight the next morning, when the phone rang. It was a three-way call from a friend and another young woman. The woman believed she was in trouble. She insisted on talking to me even though it was very late.

Lately she had been hearing a baby's voice in her ears saying, "Why am I here? Why am I here?" She was frightened and worried. I told her to calm down and be brave because she was a blessed person. "I think you are starting to wake

up as Soul," I said. I suggested that she sing HU as a love song to God and focus her inner vision in an upward direction.

Very early the next morning I called for a taxi to take me to the airport. Ten minutes before it was to arrive, the troubled woman called me again. She had been driving for over three hours to see me before I left the country. She had reached my city but was unfamiliar with the area. I gave her directions to my house.

She wanted to drive me to the airport, but I insisted she leave her car and ride with me. Once we were settled in the taxi she told me her story.

The night before, she was singing HU. She fell asleep and dreamed of a blue light and a long corridor with arches and lots of doors on both sides. A bald monk stood in the corridor.

I opened my purse and

showed her my picture of Yaubl Sacabi. He is an ECK Master who served among the ancient Mycenaeans. Now he is the guardian of the Shariyat-Ki-Sugmad, the holy ECK scriptures, in the spiritual city of Agam Des. When she said that was the man in her dream, I gave her the picture to keep. Since she had left home at 4 a.m., I thought she would be exhausted, but when I left her she was energetic and inspired.

What kind of faith and courage had made this woman drive for over three hours on winding, mountainous roads to a city she wasn't familiar with, to see a woman she'd never met? I marveled at the workings of the ECK.

Wherever I go, I share the message of Eckankar with people. I offer them HU. I tell them they are protected and loved.

Spiritual Exercise

Journey on an Ocean of Light

Tonight when you go to bed, close your eyes and locate the Spiritual Eye. It is at a point right above and between the eyebrows. Now very gently look for the Light, which can come in a number of different ways.

At first you may see just a general glow of light that you think is merely your imagination. It might appear as little blue spots of light or as a ray of light. Or it could look like a beam of light coming through an open window from the sunshine outside. The white light may also show up in any number of ways.

As you look for the Light, chant your secret word or HU (pronounced like the word *hue*), a name for God which has a power greater than the word *God* for many people. Watch as this Light turns into an ocean of light. Then, as you see It turn into an ocean, look for a little boat that's coming to shore very near where you are standing. At the helm is the Mahanta or one of the ECK Masters, who will invite you into the boat. Don't be afraid; just get in.

When you get to this point, allow any experience to follow that may. Set no limitations on it. You may end up in a video arcade, or you may end up near or inside a Temple of Golden Wisdom. Or you may have an experience of the Light and Sound of God coming directly into Soul.

Mark Daellin

Gopal Das

Dream Master of Ancient Egypt

Gopal Das

Gopal Das (*GOH-pahl DAHS*) was the Mahanta, the Living ECK Master in Egypt, 3000 BC, who founded the mystery cults of Osiris and Isis. He teaches at the Askleposis Temple of Golden Wisdom in the city of Sahasra-dal-Kanwal on the Astral Plane. There, he is the guardian of the holy book of ECK, the Shariyat-Ki-Sugmad.

Betsy White

Secret Teachings

*A*n ECKist from Africa, an electrical engineer, went to the home of a retired school principal to do some electrical work. Although the retired principal was up in years, he told the ECKist he shared his house with his father.

As they worked on the wiring together, the ECKist was telling him about ECK, when a very old man came into the room.

"Hey, what are you doing there, telling the secrets of ECK to this child?" said the old man. The child, of course, was the old man's son, the retired principal.

"They are not secret anymore," the ECKist said. "A man named Paul Twitchell brought them out to the public in 1965."

The old man thought about this for a while.

Then he said, "I first heard about Eckankar in 1914." He described the ECK Master who had taken him to a Temple of Golden Wisdom in the inner worlds, the inner heavens. "He spoke to me about Eckankar. I see this teaching has finally made it out to the earth plane."

"What did this Master look like?" the ECKist asked.

"He had long blond hair," the old man said.

"I think I know who you met. I'll bring you a picture." The ECKist went home and found a picture of Gopal Das, an ECK Master who once served as the Mahanta, the Living ECK Master—the position I fulfill today as the spiritual leader of Eckankar. He brought the picture to the old gentleman, who recognized the face immediately.

"Yes," the old man said, "that is the man who first told me about the teachings of ECK in 1914."

A strong interest in spiritual matters such as dreams or prophecy may point to one's earlier training under a Living ECK Master a long time ago.

Many people have been students of one or more ECK Masters in a past lifetime. Others may

Jason Levinson

Askleposis *(ask-leh-POH-sis)* is the Temple of Golden Wisdom on the Astral Plane, where Gopal Das, the great ECK Master, is the guardian of the fourth section of the Shariyat-Ki-Sugmad, the holy book of ECK.

be surprised to learn of an acquaintanceship with Lai Tsi, Gopal Das, Rebazar Tarzs, or another ECK Master in their dreams. Sometimes dreamers cannot put a name to their dream guide, or they get his name wrong. But the minute they see a picture of the ECK Master, they exclaim in wonder, "Why, he's been my guide for years!"

This connection exists because that ECK Master was the dreamer's beloved guide in some past era.

ECK Master Gopal Das is one such dream guide.

Merrill Peterson

Meeting the ECK Masters

Today, Gopal Das still gives spiritual aid to seekers in every part of the globe, to help them find truth.

A man had been visited by different spiritual travelers since he was a baby. It began one night when he was lying in his crib. He was about two

Ann Hubert

or three years old, and he remembers looking out the window at some stars.

Then he noticed one star that began to move sideways, first left, then right.

Suddenly the star came zooming toward Earth, right through the boy's bedroom window. It became two stars, a blue one and a white one. An instant later two spiritual travelers stood there in the bedroom. They glowed with light and goodness. They were ECK Masters who work on the inner planes to teach Soul.

One of the spiritual travelers looked at the child. "Don't be afraid," he said. "We came to you because of your love."

The boy climbed out of his crib and went to wake his parents. As he was walking toward their bed, he heard one of the spiritual travelers say, "He's not ready yet." Then they were gone.

The next time this young person ran into an

ECK Master was when he was living in Indiana as a college student. He was on his way to the library, when a very tall beggar approached him. The beggar with very clear eyes looked at the young man and said, "Excuse me, could I borrow two dollars?"

The young man had ten dollars on him. "You can have three," he said. "I only need two," the beggar replied. Then the beggar looked carefully at the young man. "In case you're interested," he said, "Paul Twitchell is giving a talk in town tonight."

"Paul Twitchell," the young man said, not recognizing the name. "What's he talking about?" The beggar told him. *This guy's some kind of spiritual nut*, the young man thought. "Uh, no thanks," he said.

He reached into his wallet and pulled out the two dollars so he could be on his way. As he handed the beggar the money, the beggar said to him, "The blessings of God, the Sugmad, are with you." And then the beggar turned and disappeared into the crowd.

The third time the young man met an ECK Master was in the dream state when he was a soldier in Vietnam. Gopal Das, an ECK Master who served years ago in Egypt during his term as the Mahanta, the Living ECK Master, took the soldier out of the body into the high planes of God every night.

They attended a spiritual study class at one of the Temples of Golden Wisdom on the inner planes, but after a time the young man got tired of these journeys. School was not his idea of spiritual adventures. Gopal Das said to him, "If you leave the class, we won't meet again." But the young man decided to explore elsewhere.

Years later the young man discovered the path of ECK. He realized then how precious the gift of meeting these ECK Masters was. As the

spiritual travelers worked with him, he had expanded his awareness of the inner worlds and developed the self-discipline that's needed to learn spiritually.

ECK Masters have quietly existed in society as agriculturists, astronomers, jewelers, painters, businesspeople, and even as sheepherders. They often adopt low-key profiles. In communities where they live, they rub shoulders with ordinary people as well as leaders of society, whose spiritual needs they attend to. It all depends on the mission of each ECK Master.

During Gopal Das's term as the Living ECK Master, the followers of ECK came to suffer much persecution. The orthodox religion and propo-

Steve Salek

nents of astrology in Egypt raised such an outcry against the ECK teachings that the ECK Masters chose to take them underground. It was to be the last time until the modern age that the teachings of the Light and Sound of God would be so available in the public forum.

Of course, the inner dream teachings of ECK never go underground. They are always available.

Touched by Divine Love

Many years ago, a teenage girl locked herself in the bathroom with the idea of ending her life with a bottle of sleeping pills. She took the pills and watched her face in the mirror. Her vision suddenly blurred. In the mirror she now saw the face of a man with blond hair and beautiful blue eyes, which were filled with tears. A single tear fell on his cheek. And with it, she sensed a mighty flow of love.

"No," he said, "it's not right to do this."

Signy Cohen

His appearance brought her to her senses. She ran from the bathroom and told her parents about the sleeping pills, and they rushed her to the hospital in time.

Years later, she recognized her guardian as the ECK Master Gopal Das. The mirror let her see into the world of love, a place unknown to her before. For had she known of it, there would certainly have been no reason to try to shorten her life. His love gave her the will to live. She thus learned about divine love.

The Golden Seed

Interest in Gopal Das today arises from his role in dreams as a primary way for one to start his search for the eternal truths that tell of the secrets of God. For it was Gopal Das who inspired the Egyptian book of dreams. He encouraged a scribe in the court of Sesostris III, an Egyptian pharaoh who reigned 1878–1843 BC, to produce it. The Egyptian book of dreams, one of the oldest books known to mankind, contains many dreams and their interpretations.

Dreams, now as then, play an important role in the teachings of ECK.

Mike had a dream, and in it he asked the ECK Master Gopal Das, "Why are there no other people in my village who know about ECK or are members of ECK?"

Gopal Das had three golden seeds in his hand. He said to Mike, "Let's put these seeds in the soil."

As he planted them, he said, "The soil is ready. But the soil and the people need to be nurtured in just the right way, and the seeds need time to grow. Each seed will grow in its own time when it's ready."

Stan Burgess

A Dream with Gopal Das

A Japanese woman who recently became an ECKist had a dream. She was riding on a bus with a few other passengers. She mentioned to the bus driver that she wanted to be let off at a certain stop.

"That's a very dangerous place at night," he cautioned her. "You don't want to get off there by yourself."

"I'll go with you," a man on the bus offered.

The ECKist and the other passenger got off the bus. They were met by a woman, a child, and one or two other people. The ECKist could see the moon in the darkening sky as they walked down the road.

Soon they came to a path that took them to a house high up in the mountains. The man from the bus opened the glass door, and they went inside.

On one wall in this house was a picture of a man with long golden hair. "Who's he?" the woman asked.

"You remember, don't you?" the man from the bus said.

All of a sudden she did remember: She had come to this mountain home many times before, on that very same bus, accompanied by the man in the picture. The dream ended at that point, but she retained a vivid memory of it.

Not long after the dream, Mike met the Regional ECK Spiritual Aide (RESA), the ECK leader in Nigeria. The RESA said, "I know someone in your town who is an ECKist; I'll get his name to you so you can meet each other."

And so this connection happened, partly through the dream state and partly through a lot of other help. The ECK brought Mike guidance on where to find someone else in his town who is a member of Eckankar.

Shortly after that she attended an ECK Satsang (spiritual study) class. Sketches of four ECK Masters were displayed on a table as part of the class discussion. As she glanced at each one, suddenly her eyes widened in surprise. "That's the man I saw in the picture in my dream!" she said, pointing to one of the sketches. It was the ECK Master Gopal Das.

Merrill Peterson

Eyes of Light

VIRGINIA REYNOLDS

Ann Hubert

It seemed my spiritual life had dried up over the past few months. I wasn't recognizing any spiritual experiences.

I was new to Eckankar and had gone to a meeting at the local ECK center. Before the meeting started, I talked with a fellow ECKist and mentioned this. "Maybe something will happen during the HU song," she said.

I knew that singing HU, the ancient name for God, aligns us with the Holy Spirit. *Perhaps she is right*, I thought.

The couch I sat on faced a wall with pictures of several ECK Masters: Gopal Das, Fubbi Quantz, Rebazar Tarzs, and Lai Tsi.

When I glanced up briefly after the HU song ended, these pictures appeared the same as before. As far as I could tell, nothing had happened during the HU song.

I continued talking with my friend. Looking up, my eyes scanned the pictures again. I stared, amazed. The picture of Gopal Das seemed to be alive—alive in the sense of molecules moving around before my eyes. And the room was suddenly brightly illuminated.

Then my eyes met those in the picture. Gopal's eyes blazed.

I continued to talk as if nothing out of the ordinary were happening. Yet, the whole time I was talking, the light from those eyes was so intense I had to avert my eyes. The light seemed to bore into my being, purifying me.

I don't remember how long this lasted or when the picture returned to normal. Just as I was leaving, though, I took one last look at Gopal Das. This time, his picture was back to normal, hanging on the wall with the others. The next week when I came back to the ECK center, the picture remained a normal picture.

After this experience, I began to look at several situations that I had refused to examine before. The light from the ECK Master's eyes had not only illuminated the room at the ECK center, but the next step in my spiritual life as well.

Betsy White

The picture of Gopal Das seemed to be alive—alive in the sense of molecules moving around before my eyes. And the room was suddenly brightly illuminated.

Spiritual Exercise

Meeting Gopal Das

Sit in an easy chair with your eyes closed, and chant the word *Gopal*. Gopal Das is one of the guardians of the Temples of Golden Wisdom. He guards the fourth section of the Shariyat-Ki-Sugmad. This is the holy book for those who follow Eckankar.

The word is chanted in two syllables. It is a sacred name and must be sung as *GOH*, then *pahl*.

Keep this up with a clear mind, and you will suddenly find yourself out of the body. You will be accompanied to the Temple of Golden Wisdom where you can listen to Gopal Das speak on the Shariyat-Ki-Sugmad.

Mark Daehlin

Lai Tsi

Chinese Sage of Wisdom

Lai Tsi

Lai Tsi (*lie TSEE*) is the Chinese ECK Master who is the guardian of the Shariyat-Ki-Sugmad on the Saguna Lok, the Etheric Plane, at the Temple of Golden Wisdom in the city of Arhirit. He once served as the Mahanta, the Living ECK Master.

Betsy White

Lai Tsi's Mission

Lai Tsi was an ECK Master who had studied religion in the schools of ancient China. He was one of the many monks who became a doctor of divinity. But at one point he came to understand that the realization of God could never be found in books. Instead, he found it in the solitude and stillness of nature.

Lai Tsi went off to a cave in the mountains up above the Yellow River in north central China. Up in the mountains he was visited by the ECK Master Tomo Geshig, one of the secret agents of a pure positive nature, who came to Lai Tsi in the Soul body for seven years before he saw him in the flesh. Lai Tsi's own Master was Yaubl Sacabi. These two ECK Masters, Yaubl Sacabi and Tomo Geshig, had been trained by Gopal Das in ancient Egypt several thousand years ago.

Signy Cohen

As Lai Tsi was readied, these ECK Masters led him into the God Worlds, heaven by heaven. There are many different levels of heaven. The Christian Bible refers to this when Jesus says, "In my father's house are many mansions," and where Saint Paul says he knew a man who had been caught up to the third heaven. And so the ECK Masters took Lai Tsi to these heavens and more.

One day, because Lai Tsi's love for God was so great, all the barriers of fear were removed and he was taken into the Light of God. He was taken to the Anami Lok, where he saw the face of God. Here he experienced the bliss and happiness which is the birthright of every Soul—of you and me. There is nothing that prevents us from having this experience except ignorance. The Light of God eventually dispels the ignorance, and the Sound of God carries us home.

When Lai Tsi awoke on the cold floor back in the cave, he found that a lion had cooled his fevered brow and that the wild deer had snuggled up against his body to give him warmth. It

Barbara Steinberg-Orlowski

now seemed as if all life, all nature, had the single-minded purpose of insuring his survival. And when he opened his eyes, he saw Tomo Geshig working in front of a roaring blaze, preparing food to nourish his body.

At this point, Lai Tsi had become the Living ECK Master. It's something one cannot talk about to anyone else. It's something no one else may recognize, except for the chosen few.

A sheepherder passing near the cave one day heard a sound like a lute. At first he thought it was one of the demons of the hills. He started to run away, but the beautiful music of the lute drew him closer. There he saw Lai Tsi sitting outside his cave. Seeing the Light of God shining from his face, the shepherd knew this was the Master who had been promised. He came nearer still; and when he had been touched, when he received the bliss of God, he went home and told the people, "The Master who has the secret of the true knowledge of God, the Light and Sound, is here among us." This is how the mission of Lai Tsi began several thousand years ago.

Lai Tsi's Prayer

"Here is a short contemplation seed which I found in myself upon returning from the heavenly worlds:

> "'**Show me Thy ways, O Sugmad;**
> **Teach me Thy path.**
> **Lead me in Thy truth, and teach me;**
> **On Thee do I wait all day.**
> **Remember, O Beloved, Thy guiding light**
> **And Thy loving care.**
> **For it has been ever Thy will,**
> **To lead the least of Thy servants to Thee!'**

"Should anyone be in distress or need to reach the great Sugmad, use this contemplation; repeat it slowly and it certainly brings results."

from "The Visions of Lai Tsi," as recorded in *The Shariyat-Ki-Sugmad*, Book Two

Betsy White

Lai Tsi

Lai Tsi is a slender man of medium height and usually wears his hair in a single braid to his shoulders. Luminous dark eyes and a wide and smiling mouth speak of benevolence and goodwill. He may appear to seekers as a silver light, along with a humming sound like that of buzzing bees.

Dick Graham

Dayaka Temple of Golden Wisdom

Dayaka Temple *(dah-YAH-kah)* is a Temple of Golden Wisdom in the city of Arhirit on the Etheric Plane. Lai Tsi is the guardian of the Shariyat-Ki-Sugmad there.

A Dream Teaching from Lai Tsi

Lai Tsi is one of Mary's favorite ECK Masters. He often appears in her dreams to teach about things like love and fear. She loves him for his strength and gentleness.

One night Mary had asked for his guidance and ended up with a potent yet frightening dream. She dreamed she had brought home an inmate. She never thought of him as a prison inmate, but simply as a human being in need of food, shelter, love, and care. Later, her suspicions about him began to mount. Why had he been in prison? As her curiosity grew,

> HE STOOD BY, GIVING HER PROTECTION, THOUGH HE LET HER HAVE A TRAUMATIC LOOK AT HOW FEAR WAS DESTROYING HER LIFE.

so did his anger and ill-treatment of her. Then he had his friends over, and they disrupted what little peace remained in her home.

She awoke in a panic. Angrily, she asked Lai Tsi how he could have allowed her to have such a frightening dream.

Then she understood its meaning.

Who was the inmate? He was a symbol for the energy current of fear she had been carrying with her for a long time. Mary had housed it, nurtured it, and slept with it, not fully aware of its basic negativity. Once she took note of its sinister force, it gained momentum and began to avenge itself upon her. Fear had always been a threat to her very existence and inner security.

All the attention she had showered upon fear had come back to her like a boomerang. It had been destroying her life. From that dream, she realized the need to get a grip on her fears if she ever wanted to find peace.

Lai Tsi had indeed been loving to her. He stood by, giving her protection, though he let her have a traumatic look at how fear was destroying her life.

"The treasures of heaven are not merely gold and silver, but the treasures of Soul—the peace, contentment, and happiness which come with the opening of the Window of Heaven. None will know this until each has a glimpse of the broad skies and the beautiful gardens, the running waters and the wonderful colors of the world beyond, by the opening of the window."

Susan Sarback

from "The Visions of Lai Tsi," as recorded in *The Shariyat-Ki-Sugmad*, Book Two

A Gift to Remember

FRAN BLACKWELL

April Munson

Just so you know that dreams are real, I have a gift for you.

When I was nine years old, I began having visits in my dreams from an old Asian man. He had a long white beard and the most beautiful eyes. They seemed to look right through me. He wore a funny little hat on his head and had a beautiful smile. Every night he would talk to me about life and explain the meaning of different things I wondered about.

One afternoon I went to a movie with my girlfriends. We were standing in line waiting to buy our tickets, laughing and being silly like normal nine-year-old girls. Suddenly I felt something. I looked past the booth where they sold the tickets. There stood the man who had been in my dreams for almost a year. When our eyes met, he nodded at me. Then he was gone.

I didn't think to turn around to my girlfriends and say, "Look at that man over there! He is the man from my dreams!" For some reason it seemed best to keep silent.

That very night he came to me again in my dreams. He said, "Tonight will be the last time I meet with you. I have to leave you now. I have to go away."

I replied, "Oh, but I'm going to miss you! I wish you didn't have to leave."

He said, "I have to do what I have to do, but just so you know that dreams are real, I have a gift for you." He placed a white plastic barrette in my hand and curled my fingers around it. Then he was gone.

When I woke up the next morning, the white barrette was really in my hand!

I began thinking about my parents, especially my mother. If she saw me with this barrette she would want to know where it came from. She wouldn't understand that a man in my dreams gave it to me. Before anyone else awoke, I snuck out of the house. I went out to the backyard, dug a hole, and buried the barrette.

But I only let go of the barrette's physical aspect. The true meaning of the gift never left me. That gift gave me the understanding of the true reality of our inner and outer lives. It proved that dreams are real.

I'll never forget the wonderful man who taught me in my dreams. At the time, I didn't know his name. Years later when I found the teachings of Eckankar, I discovered he was the ancient Chinese ECK Master Lai Tsi.

My Chinese Friend

An Aging Mother Gets a Gift from a Special Visitor

AZUCENA KURZ

At ninety-five, my mother was no longer able to make the arduous journey from her home in the Philippines to visit her children and grandchildren in the United States and Canada. She was particularly distressed when she learned that my niece (her granddaughter) was to be married in New York, surrounded by friends and family. As the wedding day drew closer, Mother became sadder and more withdrawn, refusing to eat.

Finally, weak and dehydrated, she was admitted to the hospital and soon fell into a coma. Her doctors feared she would not live to see the rest of the family return from the wedding. Another niece of mine sat by her bed, day and night, watching over her.

One morning, in the very early hours, my mother awakened and sat up, fully alert. Gently shaking my niece's shoulder, she said softly, "Go tell the doctor to come. My Chinese friend says I am fine and don't need this anymore."

She pointed to the intravenous tube in her arm.

"Lola (*grandmother* in Filipino), you need the IV," urged the doctor when he arrived, breathless, in the room. "You need it at least a

Ann Hubert

day longer so we can be sure you are adequately hydrated."

"No," insisted Mother. "My Chinese friend told me I don't need your treatment anymore! I want to go home."

Puzzled, my niece couldn't remember any Chinese visitors to my mother's bedside. But Mother was insistent. "My Chinese friend came and told me!"

Persuasive and firm, the doctor said, "I recommend you stay, Lola. But if you can drink three glasses of water in the next hour, we'll remove your IV and let you go." He thought she wouldn't be able to comply, but to everyone's surprise she not only drank the three glasses of water, but she ate her breakfast and her lunch with gusto. She was discharged from the hospital that afternoon.

I received word of this incident in Manila, where I had traveled to participate in an Eckankar regional seminar. Curious about my mother's "Chinese friend," I picked up a portrait of the Chinese ECK Master Lai Tsi before I headed home. Arriving at Mother's bedside, I sat down and showed her the picture.

As she looked at the picture, she recognized her Chinese friend. "Why, yes, that is him," she said in a dignified manner.

"Lai Tsi is an ECK Master," I replied, "a spiritual guide." A lifelong Methodist, she knew a little about Eckankar from her past visits to me in Canada. "How did you come to know him?" I asked.

"He has been my friend for a long, long time," she replied, somewhat enigmatically.

I remained home with Mother for another week, just to be sure she was OK. One morning I heard her calling to her nurse. "Hurry," she called. "Go show my Chinese friend to the door. He's just leaving." The nurse rushed to the living room and then walked back into Mother's room, looking bemused.

"There wasn't anyone there," she said. "That's because you were too slow," was Mother's disappointed reply.

Lai Tsi made several more visits after this.

My mother lived another seven years—to the age of

Jennifer Therese

"How did you come to know him?" I asked.

one-hundred-one years and nine months. When I said good-bye after my last visit in November 2001, Mother held my hands, looked deeply into my eyes, and said earnestly,

"You need not come home for my funeral." She translated (died) on February 6, 2002.

Reassured of her love and grateful for Lai Tsi's care, I didn't go home.

Recognizing Divine Love

In Johannesburg, South Africa, there is an ECKist who is very good at computer programming. He put together an ECK program for a fair in his city, a program about the ECK teachings that would be interesting to people. One of the segments had portraits of certain ECK Masters, one after another, appearing on the screen.

The children loved his presentation. They'd watch all the animated Eckankar scenes and the ECK Masters on his monitor.

One young woman came walking by and stopped at the booth. She wanted to know, "Who's that Chinese Master there?"

And Douglas, the ECKist, said, "That's Lai Tsi."

"Every time I've come past your booth, this Master happens to be on the computer," she said. "He's been my guide here in my life, and I just wondered who he was. I didn't know his name." They got to talking about the ECK Master Lai Tsi.

Lai Tsi works pretty much on the inner planes with people who have been his students in past lifetimes to prepare them to come to the path of Eckankar today. So, without knowing it, this woman was in the grasp of divine love. She was drawn to see this special computer program that Douglas had put together just because he liked to work with computers and because he wanted to give people at the fair a fresh look at the teachings of ECK. It caught her attention.

A Spiritual Exercise

A Gentle Exercise before Sleep

To travel to your inner worlds, try this spiritual exercise. Do it each evening before sleep. Shut your eyes, then sing HU (pronounced like the word *hue*) or your secret word for five or ten minutes. (A secret word comes with the Second Initiation. An individual may request this initiation after two years of study in the ECK discourses.)

Right before dozing off, say to the Mahanta, the Inner Master, "Please take me to the place where I can learn all that is good for my unfoldment. Take me to a Temple of Golden Wisdom."

Or say, "Let me see what it's like to Soul Travel; you have permission to help me."

Let a feeling of warmth and goodness fill your heart. The Mahanta is a trusted friend and companion, who loves you as you love him. Be assured of his love, protection, and guidance.

You will be safe in every way.

Fubbi Quantz

Abbot of the Katsupari Monastery

Fubbi Quantz

Fubbi Quantz (*FOO-bee KWAHNTS*) was the Mahanta, the Living ECK Master during the time of Buddha, about 500 BC. He completed his mission, then immortalized his body, and is now the guardian of the Shariyat-Ki-Sugmad at the Katsupari Monastery in northern Tibet. A teacher of Firdusi, the Persian poet, he was also the spiritual guide for Columbus and encouraged his voyage to the Americas in order to revitalize the depleted nutrition of the Europeans.

Betsy White

Fubbi Quantz Was a Seeker

Ann McGraw

Fubbi Quantz was a seeker who had this thirst for God-Realization. He was studying at a monastery, and life had put him against the rock where he couldn't see his way out. So he made a decision: I'm going to go up to the mountain. He probably figured that the mountain peak was as good a place as any to resolve the situation. He got up to the mountain peak, and he said, in effect, "God, why have you forsaken me?"

After a little while, he heard a voice that said something like, "My son, I haven't forsaken you. I have been with you through the ages." I don't have the exact words, but the lightning flashed and the thunder rolled, and from that point on he knew the meaning of the words *I am always with you.*

He had the experience of Sugmad. He had been

to the Anami, to the Ocean of Love and Mercy.

He went back down to the monastery, and the abbot who was in charge knew and understood what he had experienced and left him alone.

Fubbi Quantz went into his cell and contemplated for quite some time, at the end of which he came out and took up his mission, his responsibilities as the Mahanta, the Living ECK Master.

Abbot of the Katsupari Monastery

Fubbi Quantz is the abbot of the Katsupari Monastery in the Buika Magna Mountains of northern Tibet.

This monastery is near the Valley of Shangta, gathering place for the ECK Masters at the passing of the Rod of ECK Power. Legend has it that Jesus once went there during his "silent years" and met the ECK Abbot Fubbi Quantz, reputed to be of a remarkable age in the same body.

Chief among the writings in the Katsupari Monastery is the first section of the Shariyat-Ki-Sugmad, "The Chronicles of ECK." The Kadath Inscriptions, also found there, provide a historical record of the Living ECK Masters throughout the ages. The Records of the Kros, another set of old documents, relate the history of earth and prophesy its future.

Fubbi Quantz teaches from the sacred scriptures of the Shariyat-Ki-Sugmad, the holy book of ECK. Book One of *The Shariyat-Ki-Sugmad* was dictated by him.

Many students come to Fubbi Quantz in the dream state to study when they first begin on the path of Eckankar. He is a tall, elderly man with white hair and beard and a gentle smile. Good humor gleams in his eyes.

Stan Burgess

A Dream Class with Fubbi

*A*n ECKist, whom we'll call Nancy, awoke from a dream, giddy with excitement. At first, she couldn't remember the dream, but then it slowly came back. While traveling in the other worlds, she had met the ECK Master Fubbi Quantz.

"I haven't seen you at Katsupari in such a long time," he said. "Will you come to visit me?" She promised she would, and they parted.

Next, Nancy found herself in a garden at the Katsupari Monastery. On a whim, she decided to attend a Satsang class led by Fubbi Quantz. She slipped into his classroom and took a seat against the back wall, liking the feel of being a student. Fubbi had just told the class about a visitor from the Soul Plane. When he finished his introduction for the guest speaker, he called Nancy to the front of the room. The topic he gave her was, "Why God's Love Is Worth Anything and Everything to Attain."

Her situation struck her as humorous. She realized how quickly ECK Masters set to work

Georg Schedlbauer

any chela who accepts their invitation to visit.

Looking at the sea of expectant faces in class, she began to talk. She spoke of all the suffering that a person may endure, but how trivial it is in comparison to the happiness, majesty, and splendor of God's love. This is everywhere: in a child's hug, in a puppy's eagerness to play, and in the blooming of wildflowers on the lawn. The more we can accept divine love, the more we can receive. Yet accepting God's love is only half of it. The other part is giving it back through service.

Then she asked the class, "What can you do to serve?" This led to a spiritual discussion. Afterward, she asked them to pick a day and, at its onset, to dedicate it to ECK. Then, "See what happens."

This meeting with Fubbi Quantz was why she awoke so happy.

Resolving the Past

A woman did a spiritual exercise one night before bed and met Lai Tsi in a dream. But she forgot to ask a question that was on her mind, so the next night she went into contemplation again.

This time another ECK Master came to her from the other planes: Fubbi Quantz. He too had served as the Mahanta, the Living ECK Master centuries ago. He met her in a cave and asked her,

Betsy White

"What do you wish to know?"

She said she wanted to face the barriers between her and the next initiation. Fubbi asked her, "And what do you think they are?"

For eleven years this woman had lived with a man. About three years ago, the man had decided that he didn't want to live with her anymore, he wanted to live with someone else. So the relationship broke up, and she was bitter about the whole thing. She put practically all the responsibility for the failed relationship upon him. And she had carried this bitterness with her.

Fubbi Quantz said to her, "This is going to take seven nights, if you can come back in contemplation to this cave."

The next night she saw a previous life in which her former mate had been a child. The child had been deformed. In that life the woman had practiced smotherly love. She did everything for the child. He could do nothing for himself. In doing that, she had stopped his ability to grow spiritually. In this lifetime, she was now trying to do the same thing. This man was no longer her child as in the past. He was a grown person; he didn't want any part of it. She finally recognized her responsibility in this.

Over the next few nights she went back to the cave to meet the ECK Master Fubbi Quantz. She asked him, "How do I resolve this problem from the past?"

He said, "I'll let you go back and relive one day." So she went back and relived one day.

"How did you use your time?" he asked her.

During the day that she relived, she had let the boy do different things. She let him play a musical instrument and make his own decisions. When they played games, she let him win.

After that experience, the woman found that much of her anger had gone away.

On the seventh and last night, she met Fubbi Quantz in the cave again. This time she told the ECK Master about the anger she felt toward her father.

Fubbi Quantz said, "Let's sing HU and do a spiritual exercise."

While her eyes were still shut, Fubbi Quantz asked the woman to name two qualities about her father that she admired. She said, "That's easy. He's got a great sense of humor and a quick wit. And he has a great respect for hard work and a love for it which he passed on to me."

Fubbi Quantz wrote these two qualities on a big whiteboard with a pen that wrote in gold ink. Then he asked her, "Which two qualities of his do you greatly dislike?"

This is easy, she thought. "Number one, he's cheap." She said she had spent four hundred dollars coming out to visit him. She had spent

Merrill Peterson

seven days there, helping him paint the house, clean the house, move furniture, wash the dishes, and do other little chores. At the end of that time, he took her out to a restaurant to eat. It was the cheapest restaurant in town. Dinner—$4.50. When she started to get up and get a second helping, her father said, "No, don't do that. It's too much money."

She couldn't believe it. She decided to have dessert. He said, "No, it costs too much." And to top it off, as they were leaving, her father said, "Do you mind leaving the tip?"

Besides being so cheap, she said he was also often rude and inconsiderate. Fubbi Quantz wrote these qualities on a second whiteboard. But this time he wrote them in a light blue ink. Then he put this board behind the first one with the good qualities. He said to her, "These will someday be golden qualities, but they're not there yet."

Suddenly she understood. The anger that she'd felt toward her father vanished. She could now love her father for his good qualities. She knows that in time, as he unfolds spiritually, the rest will change too.

After these meetings of healing with the ECK Master Fubbi Quantz, the ECKist was surprised, less than a month later, to get notice from the

Merrill Peterson

Eckankar Spiritual Center that she was eligible for her next initiation.

Fubbi Quantz and the ECK Researchers

A High Initiate who works closely with an ECK Vahana (missionary) project from the ECKANKAR Spiritual Center had a vivid experience during contemplation. Wah Z, the Inner Master, took her to the Katsupari Monastery where Fubbi Quantz greeted her warmly.

Fubbi took her into an enormous room full of spiritual beings from the inner worlds and other planets. Each worked diligently. They pored over volumes of books. Some of the pages were holograms, giving a three-dimensional view of the spiritual demographics of places by layers of feelings, memories, and thoughts.

And the holograms had maps. Some maps had a few sparkling lights on them; other maps had large clusters of them.

Fraser MacDonald

Fubbi said, "The beings studying the holograms are researchers. They are pinpointing the best places to contact people who are ready for ECK."

The researchers did a thorough study of their areas. They looked at all the media. How would radio, TV, and newspapers respond to ECK in a certain area? By the way, the lights on the map were Souls that the Mahanta had already made first contact with.

Researchers also analyzed which areas had ECKists who would welcome and love the newcomers.

Fubbi added, "This is a worldwide, planetwide, innerworld-wide project. The researchers write down which media ECK Vahanas should try first and which areas would open up." A massive project.

"Reach the 33 percent who've already had an experience with the Light and Sound of God," he said.

Before leaving, Fubbi winked at her.

"In case you ever think you're doing this by yourself, remember that this is what's working behind the scenes. You're a physical vehicle, much appreciated, but it's definitely a team effort."

That was her experience during contemplation.

The entire ECK spiritual hierarchy is working on the ECK missions project. Your link with them is through the ECKANKAR Spiritual Center.

Work in harmony with the ECK, and you'll find your efforts as an ECK Vahana to be surprisingly successful.

How I Found ECKANKAR

MARGARET JACKSON

My first knowledge of Eckankar came through a small notice in the newspaper. It caught my eye because a friend of mine had recently written and mentioned he was studying this spiritual path.

I wrote to the address in the paper and received a lovely letter explaining a little about the ancient teachings of ECK.

Then I watched a video on Eckankar and began chanting the sacred ECK name for God, HU, privately at home. I wondered if it would bring any results.

Raised as a Christian, I had doubts as to whether I was dabbling in something I shouldn't. I could feel the truth of Eckankar but hesitated to venture from the familiarity of the Christian rituals.

Since childhood I had experienced a small blue dot of light upon the inner screen of my awareness and heard subtle sounds in my ears. But it never occurred to me that these were evidence of the Holy Spirit in my life. I had also been taken out of my body as a child to visit my dead grandmother and walk with her.

I thought everyone experienced such things.

I had not attended my church very often in the last ten years. What it offered always seemed to stop short of reaching God on a personal level.

One night, I sang HU. I prayed to God, Jesus, the Mahanta (the Inner Master spoken of in Eckankar), and anyone else who wanted to hear me! *Please give me a sign,* I implored silently. *Which path should I take—the path of Eckankar or the path of Christianity?* I then went to sleep.

Sometime later I awoke to see the whole of my bedroom filled with a soft, loving, golden glow.

I sat up in bed and, out of force of habit, turned on my bedside lamp. A man in a brown hooded robe stood at the foot of my bed. His eyes looked lovingly into the very soul of me, and I knew I was safe.

We spoke to each other through our minds; no outer speech was needed. The golden glow fluttered around him as he acknowledged my indecision about which path to take to spiritual awareness. Quietly he assured me that Eckankar would lead me on my own path to God-Realization. He gently reminded me to sing HU wisely and with love, and to be aware of myself as a vehicle for Divine Spirit, the ECK.

This being also communicated to me about my karma, old and new, which might lead me away from Eckankar and the Mahanta.

For about half an hour, he shared his wisdom with me. I basked in his gaze of pure love. He knew and accepted everything about me, both good and bad.

Then he smiled; his eyes twinkled and sparkled, and he was gone.

Other proof has come to me that Eckankar is the right path for me. But this was my first experience of being totally accepted. I have not seen him again, but I can still feel his gaze. Perhaps I may meet him again one day. Below left is my drawing of his face from memory.

The drawing on the left is Margaret Jackson's. To the right is an Eckankar portrait of the ECK Master Fubbi Quantz, who teaches at one of the Temples of Golden Wisdom in the inner realms. Many students of ECK study with Fubbi Quantz in the dream state or the contemplative Spiritual Exercises of Eckankar.

Visit to the World of Golden Light

At one time in the inner worlds, I was walking with the renowned ECK Master Fubbi Quantz. We were going into a world of golden light. It was a far world which had a beauty beyond description, except to say that everything there was seen through a golden veil.

There were two golden planets in the sky, and since there was no time and no space, they were moving very quickly but they weren't going anywhere. As the planets spun very fast overhead, the ECK Master Fubbi Quantz and I turned and walked further into the God World of two golden suns, but we didn't walk at all.

There was a yearning to go further and further, further than I had ever gone before, because the love of God, the Sugmad, was drawing me. At one point, Fubbi Quantz turned and said, "You have to go back now, my son." His words were spoken with a great deal

> IT WAS A FAR WORLD WHICH HAD A BEAUTY BEYOND DESCRIPTION, EXCEPT TO SAY THAT EVERYTHING THERE WAS SEEN THROUGH A GOLDEN VEIL.

of compassion and love. He spoke with the understanding of one who had experienced what I was experiencing. I knew that at one time he, like me, had wished to go on forever and that someone had said to him, "You must go back now, my son."

And so it is when you, too, have to return from the world of golden light. Whether you want to or not, you have to take the expanded consciousness which you have attained into the world of matter. The golden consciousness glows very strongly at first, then gradually it fades. Very often, there is an awful emptiness inside which says, I wish to go further into the heart of God.

It is our sense of responsibility which brings us back. The only way we can ever go further into the heart of God is to face our responsibilities to serve God. This is the paradox that both allows us to grow and gives us the yearning to want to grow.

A Spiritual Exercise

Can I Come Along?

An ECKist did a spiritual exercise one evening; she began by reading a chapter in *Stranger by the River* by Paul Twitchell called "Practice of Zikar." *Zikar* means making contact with the Holy Spirit within by chanting a holy word of God, such as HU. Singing the word *HU* is the practice of the Zikar.

The ECKist began to imagine herself in the book, being with the seeker, Peddar Zaskq, and his Master Rebazar Tarzs. She imagined herself asking permission to walk with them and listen to their conversation. Inwardly, she said, "Can I come along?" They said, "Sure."

Suddenly she found herself not in this area of her imagination but in a hallway on the inner planes. She walked down the hallway and saw a man coming toward her. He was about medium height, had a gray-and-white beard, and wore a turtleneck and sport coat. Later she identified him as the ECK Master Fubbi Quantz.

Fubbi had a set of keys in his pocket. He led the ECKist down the hallway, motioning her to hurry. They approached a door at the end of the hall, which the ECKist imagined would be opened by one of Fubbi's keys. But he walked right through the wall. This is possible because they were both in the Soul body. She followed him into a room where pearls were lying on a bed. These were pearls of wisdom.

A loud noise brought her back from the experience. She found herself back in her room, where she had begun the exercise.

This exercise is designed to help you into the higher states of consciousness so that you may become, in your own life, a greater spiritual being and one day a Co-worker with God.

Yves Beaudoin

Paul Twitchell

(Peddar Zaskq)

American Cliff Hanger
and Founder of Eckankar

Peddar Zaskq
(Paul Twitchell)

Paul Twitchell was the Mahanta, the Living ECK Master from 1965 until his translation (death) from the physical plane in 1971. He introduced the modern teachings of Eckankar to the peoples of the world through his many books, lectures, and writings. His spiritual name is Peddar Zaskq.

Betsy White

Paul Twitchell's Mission

One of the greatest things Paul Twitchell did for us was to show us what a spiritual Master is really like. This was a difficult task because the spiritual light had grown very dim. The Order of the Vairagi determined that the message of ECK was to be brought out again into the mainstream of life, so Paul Twitchell was brought forward as the Mahanta, the Living ECK Master in 1965. He came out with the ECK message and presented it simply, through his writings and his lectures.

Imagine, for a moment, what a colossal venture it must have been for Paul Twitchell to gather up the bits of ECK truth again and put them all together in one set of writings.

It took the talents of a particularly tenacious man who loved words, to cut through the red tape and get the job done.

Can you imagine yourself in his place: The spiritual hierarchy has given you the mandate to study all the religions, philosophies, and metaphysical disciplines of the world that you can get your hands on. That done, you must now compile the elements of them into an easy-to-understand set of writings.

"Your mission," says the hierarchy, "is to put these rare golden teachings into the midst of the prevailing thought among mankind today." Then the ECK Masters of the Vairagi file out of the room in silence and leave you to your own resources.

That is what happened to Paul.

The high teachings of ECK had been scattered to the four corners of the world. Though it may be

> PAUL GATHERED THE GOLDEN TEACHINGS THAT WERE SCATTERED AROUND THE WORLD AND MADE THEM READILY AVAILABLE TO US.

a strange thing to say, in this sense I see Paul as a master compiler. He gathered the golden teachings that were scattered around the world and made them readily available to us.

One thing he had in mind when presenting this message of ECK was to let the uninitiated know about it through a book; to let the people know about the Sound and Light of the ECK, of Divine Spirit. Paul, through his writings, provided tools for us. We could give someone a book such as *The Tiger's Fang*, or leave it on a park bench or in a Laundromat. Or we could put up a poster that told somebody where to find more information about the Sugmad and about the Divine Spirit, the Audible Life Current.

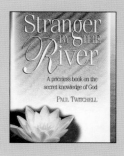

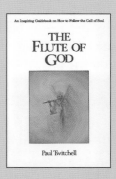

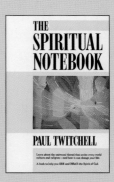

MAN HAS ALWAYS HAD THE DESIRE TO SAIL THE COSMIC SEAS AND EVENTUALLY REACH THE FAR SHORES WHERE DWELLS THE LORD OF ALL CREATION. REBAZAR TARZS, A SPIRITUAL TRAVELER, HAS FINISHED THE VOYAGE AND NOW SEEKS TO SEE THAT OTHERS HAVE THE SAME OPPORTUNITY.

PAUL TWITCHELL HAD THE EXPERIENCE OF THIS VOYAGE, AND AS SUCH REACHED MANY CONCLUSIONS AND RECORDED THEM.

MANY BELIEVE THAT THE READING OF ANY SACRED SCRIPTURE WILL BRING ONE CLOSER TO GOD, BUT THIS IS NOT SO. INDIVIDUALS MUST ADVANCE THEMSELVES IN UNDERSTANDING. NOT EVEN THE SPIRITUAL TRAVELERS COULD GIVE US THIS. WE ARE FURNISHED ONLY WITH OPPORTUNITY, AND ONLY THE EXPERIENCING OF GOD IS IMPORTANT AND DOES BRING THE SEEKER CLOSER.

Mar Amongo

An Audience with Paul Twitchell

Betsy White

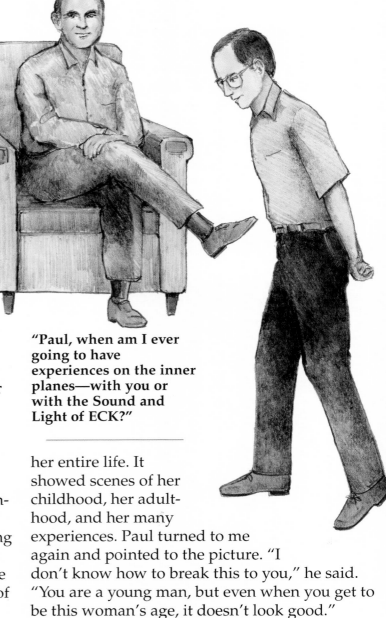

Stan Burgess

During my first year in Eckankar, I had a couple of experiences with the Light and Sound of God, the ECK; but the memory quickly faded, and I forgot about them. I began to worry, because it didn't seem that I was having any experiences.

One night as I was drifting off to sleep, I asked Sri Paul Twitchell, who was the Living ECK Master of the time, to help me. As I inwardly expressed this desire, I saw him sitting in an easy chair, watching me. I was pacing the floor in front of him, walking back and forth with my hands behind my back in the classic thinker position. And I said, "Paul, when am I ever going to have experiences on the inner planes — with you or with the Sound and Light of ECK?"

Of course, I didn't realize that it was happening. This was in the dream state, and I believed that I was wide awake. He looked at me for a long while, and then he turned his head to look at a picture of a lady. She had been on the earth plane about 199 years, and the picture showed scenes of

"Paul, when am I ever going to have experiences on the inner planes—with you or with the Sound and Light of ECK?"

her entire life. It showed scenes of her childhood, her adulthood, and her many experiences. Paul turned to me again and pointed to the picture. "I don't know how to break this to you," he said. "You are a young man, but even when you get to be this woman's age, it doesn't look good."

I knew it was all over. "Yeah," I said, "the spiritual path is too hard. It doesn't look as if I'm ever going to make any progress on this path to God at all."

Paul just sat there with his arms folded, looking at me. Finally, I walked away very much upset.

Immediately, I woke up in my bed. I was really upset, and out loud I asked the question, "When am I going to have an inner experience with the Sound and Light?"

The dream had come about so naturally that it took me nearly half a day to figure it out. The ECK Masters work in subtle ways.

Mar Amongo

When the Chela Is Ready

A soldier stationed in the Midwest responded to an inner urge to keep a dream journal. He trained himself to awaken after a dream, even if it was the middle of the night, and write the dream down. He did this night after night for months on end, when finally he realized that the dreams weren't dreams anymore. He was leaving the physical body in full consciousness and journeying into the other worlds.

The soldier carefully noted these experiences in his journal. One day, while silently reading the journal to himself, he became aware that he had never been alone in these experiences, that a presence was always with him—a spiritual being whose body glittered like a million little stars. During one experience this being took him by the hand and led him out of the body and high over the city. The being, who was a spiritual traveler, pointed to a golden structure below and told

him that it was a Temple of Golden Wisdom, where the knowledge and wisdom of the Light and Sound of God were stored and protected under the guardianship of one of the ECK Masters.

The soldier cried while reading his notes, remembering the beauty of the temple. The beauty came from the temple's very essence. The memory was very moving and uplifting to Soul.

A few years later, the soldier finished his term of military service and was returned to civilian life. One day, while browsing through a bookstore, he came upon a book that caught his attention. It was *ECKANKAR—The Key to Secret Worlds*. He picked up the book and turned it over in his hand. On the back was a photograph of the author, Paul Twitchell, whom he recognized as the being who had taken him out of the body and shown him the Temple of Golden Wisdom.

Why did he have to wait years to discover the identity of the Master who had taken him on so many wonderful journeys into the inner realms? When he was in the military, he had not been fully prepared to meet the Master. He needed more experience. He needed to overcome fear. Certain inner preparations had to be completed before the meeting could come to pass. It follows the old saying, When the chela (spiritual student) is ready, the Master appears.

Thomas E. Canny

Paul Twitchell

The First Connection

A woman from Australia had been living in a house with her fiancé for four years. Then the relationship broke up, and the woman found herself living in a dingy little apartment.

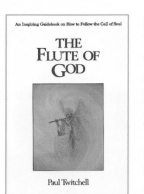

She asked the landlord if she could do something to brighten up the place, so that it would be a quiet haven to come home to. The landlord said, "Sure," so she spent time painting and cleaning up.

Many of her belongings stayed in boxes for several months. One day she decided to unpack a box of books. There in the box was *The Flute of God* by Paul Twitchell. This was before she knew anything about Eckankar. She couldn't remember buying the book; she had never seen it before. But as she held the book in her hand, she saw that the yellow cover was exactly the same color as she had just painted her apartment.

Paul Twitchell

She turned the book over, and on the back cover she saw the photo of Paul Twitchell, the ECK Master whose spiritual name is Peddar Zaskq. And she recognized him as the person who had been coming to her in her dreams for nine months.

The first time she'd seen him, she'd been asleep in her room. Suddenly she felt the presence of someone. She opened her eyes and noticed a light in her bedroom. This light grew brighter and brighter until it filled the entire room. In the center of the light stood Paul Twitchell. He came to her and put his hands above her, not touching; she could feel the power and the love of God which took away all her fears.

Finally she asked him, "Who are you? What are you doing here?" He said, "Be quiet." He was telling her to just accept the love. This was during months of hard emotional times in her life, and he came back on a few more occasions.

As she looked at the book in her hand, she said, "This man who supposedly died in 1971 came and talked with me." She wondered so much about her dream experiences that she decided to write Eckankar. But she wasn't sure whether to mail the letter.

A few days before she decided to mail the letter, Paul Twitchell came to her again. He came out of the light and said, "You now have the Light and Sound of God," and then he left.

The outer teachings of ECK cannot tailor the spiritual clothing closely enough to fit each person individually, but they do provide a gateway. They are stepping-stones into the other worlds. It's in the other worlds that you get exactly the insights, wisdom, and source of love that you need at that particular moment in your life.

God Answered My Letter!

A Stroll through a Bookstore Changes My Life

JENNIFER O'BRIEN

Jane Burgess

**"If I have a spiritual guide, I would very much like to connect
consciously with him," I wrote.**

Spring break of my final year of high school, my girlfriend Erin and I were riding a Greyhound bus bound for Toronto to visit her mother. We had been giggling and talking, when suddenly a gentleman sitting in the seat directly in front of me turned around and looked right at me. His eyes seemed to penetrate me in such a way that I became quite uncomfortable. To break his gaze, I shut my eyes and pretended to fall asleep. When at last I opened my eyes, he had turned back around—much to my relief.

After this trip I dreamed about this man. In my dreams he would knock on the back door of my parents' house. When I answered the door, he would just stand there looking at me. I had no idea who he was, but his presence was compelling.

Many years passed. I was a newly married actress, living just outside of Toronto. Since graduating from theater school, I had begun seeking answers to questions about the purpose of existence. One day I sat down at my typewriter and typed a letter to God. "If I have a spiritual guide, I would very much like to connect consciously with him," I wrote.

The church I was brought up in no longer answered my deepest questions: What am I doing here? Is heaven only for a special group? Is there such a thing as reincarnation?

I had read about reincarnation when I was younger, and it made sense to me. Why else would I have detailed dreams of places I have never been before?

Not long after I typed my note to God, I had an audition for a play. The morning of the audition I felt inspired, happy, and joyous. The monologue I chose to do was the role of a hunchbacked nun praying to Jesus. In the monologue she confides her longing to be closer to God—just the way I felt!

The audition went very well, and I left more uplifted and inspired than ever. I took a long walk to bask in the joyous moment and wandered into an old, nondescript secondhand bookstore. All at once I knew that I must have a book about Soul!

I walked to a bookshelf, and there it was, right in front of me—*In My Soul I Am Free*. It was about the teachings of Eckankar. It told me that I am Soul and have a very distinct purpose for being here: to become a Co-worker with God. It spoke of the Living ECK Master, the spiritual leader of Eckankar, who guides students both outwardly and inwardly in dreams and through the

Spiritual Exercises of ECK.

After I read the book, I did a spiritual exercise it suggested for contacting the Light and Sound of God. I sat on the floor in my bedroom and put my attention lightly on my Third Eye—the spot between my eyebrows—and sang HU, a love song to God. After a few minutes, I began to hear a very high-pitched humming sound. It occurred to me that I had been hearing this sound since I was a little girl, lying in bed at night! When I had asked my mother about it, she had simply replied that it was the Sound of Silence. The sound had always brought me comfort and a feeling of belonging.

A short time later, I examined the photograph of Paul Twitchell, the modern-day founder of Eckankar, on the back cover of the book. I recognized his eyes. It was Paul who had appeared to me that day on the Greyhound bus and later in my dreams. The presence of the Mahanta had been with me all along, preparing me for the spiritual training that was to come into my life twelve years later.

At last my questions were answered. I knew that I could turn to

this very special Master for the spiritual direction and guidance I had been longing for. My letter to God had been answered!

I became a member of Eckankar with no hesitation. I had complete trust that my questions had answers. Now each day presents me with the opportunity to love and grow to my fullest spiritual potential.

All at once I knew that I must have a book about Soul!

Spiritual Exercise

The Easy Way

Just before sleep, place attention upon your Spiritual Eye. It is between the eyebrows. Then sing HU or God silently.

Fix attention on a blank movie screen in your inner vision, and keep it free of any pictures. If unwanted mental thoughts, images, or pictures do flash up on the screen of your imagination, replace them with the face of the Living ECK Master.

After a few minutes of silence, you may hear a faint clicking sound in one ear, perhaps like the sound of a cork popping from a bottle. You will find yourself in the Soul form in a most natural way, looking back at your physical body in bed.

Now, would you like to go on a short outing?

There is nothing to fear, for no harm can come to you while outside the body. The Mahanta will be with you to keep watch over your progress and offer support. After a while, the Soul body will return and slide gently into the physical self.

That is all there is to it.

If this exercise is not successful the first time, try it again later. The technique works. It has worked for many others.

Claude Gruffy

Harold Klemp

(Wah Z)

The Mahanta, the Living ECK Master—
a Modern Prophet

Sri Harold Klemp

Harold Klemp is the present Mahanta, the Living ECK Master. He received the Rod of ECK Power at midnight of October 22, 1981, in the Valley of Shangta at the Oracle of Tirmer, under the direction of Rebazar Tarzs, the Torchbearer of Eckankar. As the spiritual head of Eckankar, he brings new life and hope to thousands for a better, more direct way to God. His spiritual name is Wah Z, or Z.

Sri Harold Klemp, the Mahanta, the Living ECK Master

Robert Huntley

The Experience of God

In 1970, I was blessed with the wave of ECK love that changed my life forever. It was the shattering experience of God-Realization.

Susan Sarback

Of course, I did not know what it was then, and in the years from then until 1981, when I took the Rod of ECK Power, all kinds of fulfillments of the God State came to me by degrees. All these degrees of fulfillment had as their origin the primordial wave of Shabda, Voice of the Sugmad.

When the Shabda Dhun, the ECK, swept over me on a lonesome bridge near midnight of a cold night in early spring, It was a thundering, crashing wave that was too great for my karma-ridden body to bear. The purification of the Shabda brought me horrible pain, a pain so deep and complete that it is beyond description, for it was both terrible and exquisite at once.

In the years since 1970, I have learned the secret of opening the inner channel to let the ECK love come through at will. No longer is it necessary to wait for the rare occasions when the bruises of life can temporarily soften me so the Voice of God comes through in all Its splendor.

Now It comes when I use the secret method of letting It come to me. It is there for comfort, healing, and joy. In the ability to drink of the pure love of God is the meaning of the term "the God-intoxicated man."

Temple of ECK
Chanhassen, Minnesota

The guardian of the Temple of ECK in Chanhassen is the Living ECK Master. The Temple is a gathering place for inner and outer study. Seekers of truth come here physically, in the dream state, in contemplation, and via Soul Travel to study the holy works of ECK.

Robert Huntley

Spiritual Exercise: Temple Technique

One of the Temples of Golden Wisdom here on the physical plane is the Temple of ECK in Chanhassen, Minnesota. Any of you who visit will find that it has a special character, a presence of its own. That presence is the love of God.

Go there with an open mind, without any ideas or notions about what this presence should be. Look around, listen to the tour guide, and just be there.

Later, if you are ever in need of spiritual help, imagine yourself back at the Temple.

Do this at some quiet time—in your private moments of contemplation or at bedtime. Ask the question that is on your mind, that you need help with, and then just go to sleep. Often you'll wake up in the morning with an entirely different view of the situation.

Robert Huntley

Cynthia Samul

When You Hear the Sound

A woman traveled to the Temple of ECK and was very excited about attending an ECK Worship Service. But sitting in the sanctuary, she couldn't contemplate. There were too many people around. After the service she decided to take a tour of the Temple. When they got to the chapel, the tour guide said to the group, "You look so comfortable. If you like, we'll just stay here a while and contemplate."

When they sat down, the woman all of a sudden heard the sound of chanting, the way monks used to chant in monasteries centuries ago. *Why would they pipe in music like that?* she wondered. She looked around for the speakers, but there weren't any. Suddenly she realized the chanting was coming from within her. She was hearing ECK Masters singing.

Often when people hear a certain sound in a place like that, they're making a connection with their past, with a time when they made great strides in a spiritual way. At a time in the past, in a monastery, this individual was making progress spiritually and gave this love for God that has carried subconsciously into this lifetime. She came to the Temple and in contemplation in the chapel heard this chanting. She first wondered what it was, then realized she was hearing the Sound of ECK. This is one of the ways you may hear It.

Doors of HU

I would like to give you a spiritual exercise called the Doors of HU. In contemplation tonight, visualize two front doors of the Temple of ECK in Chanhassen, Minnesota. On the left door see a big golden *H* and on the right door a big golden *U*. In contemplation, walk to the doors while chanting HU, pull them open slowly, and go inside.

See what the Mahanta, the Living ECK Master wants to show you. Whatever is there is for your spiritual unfoldment. You may find it to be an enjoyable piece of wisdom or insight into life. Often you'll be shown a way to see the HU as It manifests in the activities of people around you.

People singing softly to each other, the song is of the HU. People laughing, the laughter is of the HU. And even when there are people crying, the crying is of the HU. The falling rain, its sound is of the HU. And the birds, and the wind. These are all of the sound of HU.

Rick McDiarmid

The Sound Room

Dawn Meadaer

An ECKist was going through a great period of depression, and one morning she felt it would be a good idea to write an initiate report. The initiate report allows Divine Spirit to begin working things out. But she became so depressed as she was writing that she couldn't even get through the letter. So she quit.

She went into contemplation and found herself on the inner planes with Wah Z, the Inner Master. He took her to a room in a beautiful Temple of Golden Wisdom. He said, "This is the Sound room. Would you like a Sound healing?"

The ECKist said, "Sure."

Wah Z told her to climb up on a large stone table. As she lay there, she began to feel the Sound Current of ECK coming through. It felt very soothing, as if all her inner bodies were being massaged.

Soon she was calm and relaxed. As the transformation took place, the depression began to leave her.

Then she sensed the Sound Current raising her from the table. She was lifted up to the ceiling and out through a small opening into the higher states where the Sound Current was much more refined. She felt the remainder of her depression gradually leaving her, until it was gone. She came out of the short contemplation feeling completely changed.

The exercise helped her because she had done as much as she could on her own first. The initiate report she had started to write was the trigger that opened her consciousness. She was able to accept the nudge to go into contemplation.

In contemplation, the Mahanta could take her to an inner temple of healing. There the Sound Current, which is the Voice of God, could directly enter her inner bodies and begin to put them into balance. The balance always starts on the inner planes, then works its way out to the physical plane.

Life may be difficult for her tomorrow, but now the woman knows about the Sound room in the Temple of Golden Wisdom. She can ask to go there anytime.

Visit Temples in Your Dreams

In the dream state or during Soul Travel, the seeker is accompanied to one of the temples by an ECK Master, such as Rebazar Tarzs, Peddar Zaskq (Paul Twitchell's spiritual name), or Wah Z (my spiritual name).

There the seeker can read from one of the books of the Shariyat-Ki-Sugmad. This is part of the ECK path. There are two volumes of the Shariyat in print here on earth, but many more are kept in the other temples on the inner planes. Its books tell the story of Soul's many lives on earth and in the other worlds. Sometimes the human mind cannot contain what the individual takes in while traveling in the Soul body. But even if he doesn't remember what he has read, the golden truth is within him.

Though the temples on the lower planes are usually located in a building of some kind, on the Soul Plane and higher there is no such structure. Here you find the action of the Sound and Light working directly with you as Soul, coming into you to uplift and give the knowledge and wisdom to which your state of consciousness entitles you. Here it is impossible to speak of what you take in, because there simply are no words for it.

Gary Cooper

In the three accounts that follow, students of Eckankar tell of their experiences meeting the Mahanta, the Living ECK Master and of being helped by him.

Soul Travel to the Temple of ECK

TAIWO OTITOLAIYE

I had made a vow to be at the Temple of ECK when it opened. I kept this in mind for a very long time, but as the day drew nearer, I forgot my promise.

Then one morning I awoke from a wonderful dream. In my dream, I was in a large hall that looked like an auditorium. Many people were gathered there. Some were seated, while others

looked for seats. They all wore smiling faces, a sign of the presence of divine love. Then Sri Harold Klemp, the Mahanta, the Living ECK Master, was standing in front of the gathering. I was overwhelmed with joy listening to the Master as he spoke about the Light and Sound of God.

In my dream, I walked out of the building to look at the surroundings. I was baffled because the building seemed to be a permanent home for Eckankar. In the past I had been used to attending seminars at rented buildings.

When I awoke, it did not occur to me that this had been the Temple of ECK at Chanhassen. I did not realize it until two days later when I received a mailing from Eckankar. There in the mailing was a picture of the Temple of ECK—the very building I had Soul Traveled to in my dreams.

Barbara Moss

Jackie Flatow

Spare Change

A Homeless Woman Gives Me an Unexpected Gift

TWEED CONRAD

You got any spare change?" The voice came from a young woman sitting on the sidewalk on the Berkeley street corner where I was waiting for the walk signal.

To take my mind off an impending migraine headache, I could've gone to a movie, gone home to nurse my migraine, or served Divine Spirit by putting up flyers on the university campus for an upcoming Eckankar seminar in San Francisco. I had chosen to put up flyers. I had only three flyers left and was headed to a nearby juice bar to quench my thirst.

I turned to examine the owner of the voice. She didn't look like the usual street-corner panhandler. Her clear blue eyes and smiling countenance belied her circumstances.

Instead of spare change, I handed her a seminar flyer, briefly told her about Eckankar, and turned to cross the street.

"Oh, I know this man. I've met him."

I turned back to find her looking intently at the photo of Harold Klemp on the flyer.

"Yes, that's him," she continued. "He lives in Oakland or somewhere around here, doesn't he?"

"Well, actually, he lives in Minnesota. But he comes to people all over the world in times of need. How did you meet him?"

The young woman, whose name was Rainbow, told me her harrowing story. Two men had abandoned her in a dangerous part of Oakland after trying to take what little money she had. She had been terrified they would return to harm her.

Frozen with fear and confusion, she had cowered in the street, paralyzed, not knowing where to go or what to do next. Suddenly a man had appeared from nowhere. "God is always with you," he had said. "You are never alone."

He warned her she was in grave danger where she was. "You need to find a bus and get to a safer area."

His intervention broke her paralysis. She had caught a bus back to Berkeley, ending up on my street corner. "After he left," Rainbow added, "I thought to myself, *He's a really nice person. I bet he loves animals.*"

"Yes, he does indeed."

By now I was sitting beside her on the sidewalk, smiling and nodding at everything she said.

"What's his name? I forgot."

"Harold Klemp."

"No, that's not it."

"Sri Harold?" I ventured.

"No."

"Harji?" No again. Maybe he had given her his spiritual name.

"Wah Z?" I finally asked.

"Yes, that's it," she said, relieved. "What was that name again?"

"Wah Z."

"Yes." She appeared to be absorbed in the memory of that moment—the sound and sight of Wah Z's presence.

A bright light shone all around her. She had indeed been touched by Divine Spirit, and I felt honored to be a witness to her linkup with the Mahanta, the Living ECK Master. Rainbow had indeed been a colorful gift from God on a gray street corner. When I finally bid her good-bye and continued on my way, I realized with gratitude that by choosing service I had experienced a day of divine love. And my migraine had failed to manifest! I have not had one since.

"Wah Z Caught Me"

ANNIE TOWHILL

Robert Huntley

A seriously ill relative was coming to stay with us. The bedroom she was going to use was on the second floor, but her special bed was just too big to carry upstairs. The only way to bring it up was through a sliding glass door in our second-floor bedroom. This door is usually locked because there is no porch or balcony outside—just an eight-foot drop to the ground.

We had put a small picnic table below the door to stand on as the bed was lifted through the doorway. Half the family was outside; the rest of us stood in the upstairs bedroom talking, waiting for the bed.

Suddenly my three-year-old son, Trevan, who had been taking a bath, came running naked into the room. With a gasp I realized where he was headed—right for the open door! He was expecting the door to be shut, so he could lean up against the glass and see Grandpa outside.

I lunged after him. If he had been dressed, I would have caught him. But just as my fingertips touched his skin, he flew out the door with me right behind him. I was stopped abruptly by my sister's grip on my belt.

My heart felt like it was being torn apart. I had been so close but still unable to prevent my son from falling.

Pandemonium broke out.

We all ran down the stairs.

When I got outside, my father was holding Trevan. He hadn't seen Trevan fall. The only injury was a bloody nose.

No one could explain why Trevan wasn't badly injured.

The next day I discovered the real reason. I asked Trevan why he didn't get hurt any worse.

To my amazement he said, "Wah Z caught me." Wah Z is the spiritual name of the Mahanta, the Living ECK Master. I now understood the extent of the protection of the Mahanta.

Claude Gruffy

River Run to God

A woman went to sleep and woke up on the inner planes. In the dream state she had a raft, and she was using a pole to push it along in the shallow water, before moving into the current of a wild river. She was just ready to push off when the Mahanta came along.

"What are you doing?" the Mahanta called.

"I'm going down the river," she answered.

"Would you like some help?" he asked.

"Sure."

"I mean, do you really want help?" he asked again.

"Yes, I really would like to have some help," she said.

"All right," the Mahanta said. "If you really want help, we'll build a house on your raft."

"A house?" she said in alarm. "Won't the raft tip over with a house on it?"

"No," he answered, "it will give it ballast."

The woman hesitated. She had never heard the word *ballast* before. Later, when she looked in a dictionary, she found that it meant something that gives stability.

"But I don't know how to build a house," she said, finally.

"Don't worry, I'll help."

SHE LOOKED AROUND THE RAFT AND FELT COMFORTABLE, KNOWING THAT AS SHE HEADED DOWN THE RIVER, THE MAHANTA WOULD BE THERE TO HELP HER AROUND THE BLIND BENDS.

The Mahanta brought lumber. "I'll cut it to size, and you hammer it in place," he said. "I'll show you where."

They worked together floor by floor, wall by wall, and room by room at her own speed, which was slow and unsure, until the house was finally finished. Then they climbed on board. "Let's go!" the Master said cheerfully.

She looked around the raft and felt comfortable, knowing that as she headed down the river, the Mahanta would be there to help her around the blind bends.

As the woman began her study of the ECK discourses, she became more aware of the inner worlds. When she made the inner commitment to the path of ECK, the Master told her to build a raft on the inner planes for her journey home to God. When she was ready to push off, she was frightened of this voyage to forever, and so the Master helped her build a house, which would make the raft more secure.

The house was the knowledge of ECK that she would need in order to survive the river run to God.

On the inner planes, ECK Masters appear to

Rick McDiarmid

people in a way they can understand, to offer the wisdom of the ages. The ECK writings tell countless stories of people like you who've met Rebazar Tarzs or another of the ECK Masters. The role of these Masters is to bring spiritual upliftment to all.

When all spiritual conditions are in order, one or another ECK Master will appear and bring you blessings from the Most High.

Cynthia Samul

You and the ECK Teachings

There are two sides to the ECK teachings—the inner and the outer. The outer teachings come from the outer person—the Living ECK Master. As such, he writes discourses, articles, and gives talks. On the inner side—the greater side—the Mahanta appears as counterpart to the Living ECK Master, helping people in the dream state. Here the Mahanta is also known as the Dream Master.

The Inner Master and the Outer Master are, of course, one and the same: the Mahanta, the Living ECK Master. It is important to understand that the Master is one being.

The Outer Master provides the books and teachings of ECK to acquaint you with the elements of the whats, wheres, and whys of the boundless inner worlds. He does this to inform you of the endless possibilities of unfoldment on the inner planes.

The inner teachings will fit you like custom-made clothing of the finest material. No outer teaching could ever do so. There are dozens of limitations upon the outer teachings, like the language of a chela (spiritual student) and his level of literacy.

My mission is to introduce the high teachings of ECK into the everyday lives of people.

I continue to sit down at my desk to write the ECK articles and letters to help you spiritually. Yet it is necessary to address you as part of a group consciousness. In other words, I have to determine the strongest pulse of the ECK audience to answer your spiritual needs. Then I speak to your heart, a one-on-one communication. At best, however, this approach can only address the general needs of any one individual.

Still, this approach is successful. It shows you how to reach the Inner Master, who can tailor the inner teachings to your spiritual needs.

The Inner Master welcomes you in the dream state and speaks to you like an old friend. He offers the spiritual help most appropriate that very hour. It certainly is a claim that no pastor, priest, or rabbi would dare to make. Help for the hour is truly one of the chief benefits of the inner teachings of ECK. My talks and writings tell story upon story of people who've met the ECK Masters in their dreams and so discovered a gold mine rich with countless nuggets of true value.

Belief in the Master's ever-present company relies upon an individual's degree of unfoldment. Actual inner experiences help one move to a greater understanding of the ways of divine revelation.

The ECK Masters all strive to help others—and especially you—reach God-Realization too. And thereby the capacity to give and receive vastly more love.

Moreover—and this is important—you can learn to become a Co-worker with God here and now, while still on earth.

Spiritual help is always there for the asking.

Spiritual Exercise

Meeting the Master

Take a comfortable sitting position on your bed or in a chair. Gaze gently and sweetly into the Spiritual Eye between the eyebrows.

Everything may appear dark for a moment. Gaze into the space between the brows minutely and more minutely. Look for the Light, a sheet of white light.

Shirley Cean Youngs

The Light may be like a great sun, throwing Its glittering, brilliant rays in a circle around you, Its brilliancy greater than ten thousand suns.

Suddenly you realize that the Light is coming from within yourself, spreading into an ever-widening circle until It fills the whole universe. It flows out of a center within you and becomes a burning beacon. Feel your whole body pulse with the rhythm of Its surging waves like the pounding of surf upon a sandy beach.

You hear the roaring of the surf in your ears, and it grows and grows. Suddenly into your inner vision steps the Mahanta, the Living ECK Master. Greet him with joy in your heart and begin your journey into the worlds of God.

What Is
ECKANKAR?

What Is Eckankar?

*E*ckankar is among the new religions, which make up a little more than 2 percent of the world's population. However, this group is growing in both size and importance.

The teachings of ECK define the nature of Soul more carefully than do other current religions. You are Soul, a particle of God sent into the worlds (including earth) to gain spiritual experience. The goal in ECK is spiritual freedom in this lifetime, after which you become a Co-worker with God, both here and in the next world. Karma and reincarnation are primary beliefs.

Key to the ECK teachings is the Mahanta, the Living ECK Master. He has the special ability to act as both the Inner and Outer Master for ECK students. He is the prophet of Eckankar, given respect but not worship. He teaches the sacred name of God, HU, which lifts you spiritually into the Light and Sound of God, the ECK (Holy Spirit). Purified by the practice of the Spiritual Exercises of ECK, you are then able to accept the full love of God in this lifetime.

Personal experience with the Light and Sound of God is the cornerstone of Eckankar. Of all the religions on Earth today, Eckankar offers the most direct teachings on the Light and Sound of God. These twin pillars are missing in whole or in part from the rest. People who truly find these two aspects of God undergo a complete spiritual change. Life becomes fresh and new again, as it was in early childhood.

When the student is ready, the Master appears.

The Mahanta often comes first in his radiant body, which shimmers like so many twinkling stars. Such inner experiences occur more often and with more vividness in ECK than in possibly any other spiritual path on earth, because this teaching pulses with the actual Light and Sound of God as its dynamic, living elements.

The Spiritual Exercises of ECK are the lost passkey to life. They give the secrets of the ancient ones.

So continue with the Spiritual Exercises of ECK to open your heart to this Spirit of Life. Then you may also see the Light of God. Perhaps shortly, you'll also be privileged to hear the delightful melody of God's Voice, the ancient and holy Sound.

The teachings of ECK show you how to find the presence of God.

Glossary

Words set in SMALL CAPS are defined elsewhere in this glossary.

ECK. *EHK*   The Life Force, the Holy Spirit, or Audible Life Current which sustains all life.

ECKANKAR. *EHK-ahn-kahr*   Religion of the Light and Sound of God. Also known as the Ancient Science of SOUL TRAVEL. A truly spiritual religion for the individual in modern times. The teachings provide a framework for anyone to explore their own spiritual experiences. Established by PAUL TWITCHELL, the modern-day founder, in 1965. The word means "Co-worker with God."

ECK MASTER(s).   Spiritual Masters who can assist and protect people in their spiritual studies and travels. The ECK Masters are from a long line of God-Realized SOULs who know the responsibility that goes with spiritual freedom.

HU. *HYOO*   The most ancient, secret name for God. The singing of the word *HU* is considered a love song to God. It can be sung aloud or silently to oneself.

LIVING ECK MASTER.   The title of the spiritual leader of ECKANKAR. His duty is to lead SOUL back to God. The Living ECK Master can assist spiritual students physically as the Outer Master, in the dream state as the Dream Master, and in the spiritual worlds as the Inner Master.

MAHANTA. *mah-HAHN-tah*   A title to describe the highest state of God Consciousness on earth, often embodied in the LIVING ECK MASTER. He is the Living Word. An expression of the Spirit of God that is always with you. Sometimes seen as a Blue Light or Blue Star or in the form of the Mahanta, the Living ECK Master.

SHARIYAT-KI-SUGMAD. *SHAH-ree-aht-kee-SOOG-mahd*   The sacred scriptures of ECKANKAR. The scriptures are comprised of about twelve volumes in the spiritual worlds. The first two were transcribed from the inner PLANES by PAUL TWITCHELL, modern-day founder of ECKANKAR.

SOUL.   The True Self. The inner, most sacred part of each person. Soul exists before birth and lives on after the death of the physical body. As a spark of God, Soul can see, know, and perceive all things. It is the creative center of Its own world.

SOUL TRAVEL.   The expansion of consciousness. The ability of SOUL to transcend the physical body and travel into the spiritual worlds of God. Soul Travel is taught only by the LIVING ECK MASTER. It helps people unfold spiritually and can provide proof of the existence of God and life after death.

SOUND AND LIGHT OF ECK.   The Holy Spirit. The two aspects through which God appears in the lower worlds. People can experience them by looking and listening within themselves and through SOUL TRAVEL.

SPIRITUAL EXERCISES OF ECK.   The daily practice of certain techniques to get us in touch with the Light and Sound of God.

SRI. *SREE*   A title of spiritual respect, similar to reverend or pastor, used for those who have attained the Kingdom of God. In ECKANKAR, it is reserved for the MAHANTA, the LIVING ECK MASTER.

SUGMAD. *SOOG-mahd*   A sacred name for God. Sugmad is neither masculine nor feminine; It is the source of all life.

TEMPLES(s) OF GOLDEN WISDOM.   These Golden Wisdom Temples are spiritual temples which exist on the various PLANES—from the Physical to the Anami Lok; CHELAS of ECKANKAR are taken to the temples in the SOUL body to be educated in the divine knowledge; the different sections of the SHARIYAT-KI-SUGMAD, the sacred teachings of ECK, are kept at these temples.

WAH Z. *WAH zee*   The spiritual name of SRI HAROLD KLEMP. It means the Secret Doctrine. It is his name in the spiritual worlds.

For more explanations of ECKANKAR terms, see *A Cosmic Sea of Words: The ECKANKAR Lexicon* by Harold Klemp.

For more information about Eckankar, or to request Eckankar materials by phone, using a credit card, call (952) 380-2222, 8:00 a.m.–5:00 p.m., central time, Monday through Friday. Or write: ECKANKAR, PO Box 2000, Chanhassen, MN 55317-2000 USA. Visit Eckankar's Web site at www.Eckankar.org.

For Further Reading and Study

Those Wonderful ECK Masters

Harold Klemp

Could you be one of the countless people who have been touched by a meeting with an ECK Master? These real-life stories and spiritual exercises can awaken you to the presence and help of these spiritual guides. Since the beginning of time they have offered guidance, protection, and divine love to help you fulfill your spiritual destiny.

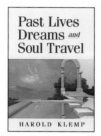

Past Lives, Dreams, and Soul Travel

Harold Klemp

What if you could recall past-life lessons for your benefit today? What if you could learn the secret knowledge of dreams to gain the wisdom of the heart? Or Soul Travel, to master the shift in consciousness needed to find peace and contentment? To ride the waves of God's love and mercy? Let Harold Klemp, leading authority in all three fields, show you how.

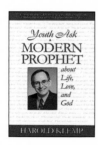

Youth Ask a Modern Prophet about Life, Love, and God

Harold Klemp

What am I here for? How do I find lasting love? When will my karma be finished? Do these questions sound familiar? The youth of today aren't afraid to voice these important questions, and many more, to Harold Klemp. His answers are candid and wise with practical solutions. You will find great value in this book no matter your age.

How to Survive Spiritually in Our Times,
Mahanta Transcripts, Book 16

Harold Klemp

A master storyteller, Harold Klemp weaves stories, tips, and techniques into the golden fabric of his talks. They highlight the deeper truths within you, so you can apply them in your life *now*. He speaks right to Soul. It is that divine, eternal spark that you are. The survivor. Yet survival is only the starting point in your spiritual life. Harold Klemp also shows you how to gain in spiritual wealth. This book's a treasure.

The Tiger's Fang

Paul Twitchell

Paul Twitchell's teacher, Rebazar Tarzs, takes him on a journey through vast worlds of Light and Sound, to sit at the feet of the spiritual Masters. Their conversations bring out the secret of how to draw closer to God—and awaken Soul to Its spiritual destiny. This book, with its vivid descriptions of the heavenly worlds and citizens, is also available as a graphic novel.

Available at bookstores, online booksellers, or directly from Eckankar: www.Eckankar.org; (952) 380-2222; ECKANKAR, Dept. BK62, PO Box 2000, Chanhassen, MN 55317-2000 USA.

About the Author

Author Harold Klemp is known as a pioneer of today's focus on "everyday spirituality." Raised on a Wisconsin farm, he attended divinity school before serving in the U.S. Air Force.

In 1981, after years of training by the ECK Masters, he became the spiritual leader of Eckankar, Religion of the Light and Sound of God. His mission is to help people find their way back to God in this life.

Harold Klemp speaks each year to thousands of seekers at Eckankar seminars. Author of more than fifty-five books, he continues to write, including many articles and spiritual-study discourses. His inspiring and practical approach to spirituality helps thousands of people worldwide find greater freedom, wisdom, and love in their lives.